SELECT PO

OF

OLIVER GOLDSMITH.

EDITED, WITH NOTES,

BY

WILLIAM J. ROLFE, A.M.,

FORMERLY HEAD MASTER OF THE HIGH SCHOOL, CAMBRIDGE, MASS.

WITH ENGRAVINGS.

NEW YORK:

HARPER & BROTHERS, PUBLISHERS,

FRANKLIN SQUARE.

1887.

ENGLISH CLASSICS.

EDITED BY WM. J. ROLFE, A.M.

Illustrated.   16mo, Cloth, 56 cents per volume ; Paper, 40 cents per volume.

SHAKESPEARE'S WORKS.

The Merchant of Venice.
Othello.
Julius Cæsar.
A Midsummer-Night's Dream.
Macbeth.
Hamlet.
Much Ado about Nothing.
Romeo and Juliet.
As You Like It.
The Tempest.
Twelfth Night.
The Winter's Tale.
King John.
Richard II.
Henry IV.   Part I.
Henry IV.   Part II.
Henry V.
Richard III.
Henry VIII.
King Lear.

The Taming of the Shrew.
All 's Well that Ends Well.
Coriolanus.
The Comedy of Errors.
Cymbeline.
Antony and Cleopatra.
Measure for Measure.
Merry Wives of Windsor.
Love's Labour 's Lost.
Two Gentlemen of Verona.
Timon of Athens.
Troilus and Cressida.
Henry VI.   Part I.
Henry VI.   Part II.
Henry VI.   Part III.
Pericles, Prince of Tyre.
The Two Noble Kinsmen.
Venus and Adonis, Lucrece, etc.
Sonnets.
Titus Andronicus.

GOLDSMITH'S SELECT POEMS.
GRAY'S SELECT POEMS.

PUBLISHED BY HARPER & BROTHERS, NEW YORK.

☞ *Any of the above works will be sent by mail, postage prepaid, to any part of the United States, on receipt of the price.*

PREFACE.

THE plan of this little book is similar to that of my edition of *The Merchant of Venice* and other of Shakespeare's plays.

The text is based on Cunningham's, which is the most accurate of the recent editions. This has been carefully collated with Prior's, Corney's, and the "Globe" edition, and also with many of the early editions, for which I have been especially indebted to the Harvard College Library and to the Athenæum and Public Libraries of Boston. Among these are the 1st, 3d, 4th, and 13th editions of *The Traveller*, the 1st. 4th, and 7th (an *American* reprint in quarto, published at Springfield, Mass., 1783) of *The Deserted Village*, and the 4th of *Retaliation*.

The 13th edition of *The Traveller* (in the Athenæum library) contains some readings, including one entire couplet (see note on line 374), which I have found in no other edition, early or recent. This edition is un-dated, and bears no name of publisher or printer. The title-page is as follows: "The Traveller, or, A Prospect of Society. A Poem. By Dr. Goldsmith. The thirteenth edition. London: Printed for the Booksellers in Town and Country."

The notes are fuller than in any other edition known to me. Many of them are original; the rest have been drawn from every accessible source, credit being given in all cases where justice to others or to myself seemed to require it.

Cambridge, July 30, 1875.

CONTENTS.

STATUE OF GOLDSMITH.—[BY J. H. FOLEY.]

OLIVER GOLDSMITH.—[FROM A PAINTING BY SIR JOSHUA REYNOLDS.]

OLIVER GOLDSMITH.

By Thomas Babington Macaulay.

Oliver Goldsmith was one of the most pleasing English writers of the eighteenth century. He was of a Protestant and Saxon family which had been long settled in Ireland, and which had, like most other Protestant and Saxon families, been in troubled times harassed and put in fear by the native population. His father, Charles Goldsmith, studied in the reign of Queen Anne at the diocesan school of Elphin, became attached to the daughter of the schoolmaster, married her, took orders, and settled at a place called Pallas in the County of Longford. There he with difficulty supported his wife and children on what he could earn, partly as a curate and partly as a farmer.

At Pallas Oliver Goldsmith was born in November, 1728. That spot was then, for all practical purposes, almost as remote from the busy and splendid capital in which his later years were passed as any clearing in Upper Canada or any sheep-walk in Australasia now is. Even at this day those enthusiasts who venture to make a pilgrimage to the birth-place of the poet are forced to perform the latter part of their journey on foot. The hamlet lies far from any high-road, on a dreary plain, which in wet weather is often a lake. The lanes would break any jaunting-car to pieces; and there are ruts and sloughs through which the most strongly built wheels cannot be dragged.

When Oliver was still a child his father was presented to a living worth about £200 a year in the County of West-meath. The family accordingly quitted their cottage in the wilderness for a spacious house on a frequented road, near the village of Lissoy. Here the boy was taught his letters by a maid-servant, and was sent in his seventh year to a vil-lage school kept by an old quartermaster on half-pay, who professed to teach nothing but reading, writing, and arith-metic, but who had an inexhaustible fund of stories about ghosts, banshees, and fairies, about the great Rapparee chiefs, Baldearg O'Donnell and galloping Hogan, and about the ex-ploits of Peterborough and Stanhope, the surprise of Mon-juich, and the glorious disaster of Brihuega. This man must have been of the Protestant religion; but he was of the ab-original race, and not only spoke the Irish language, but could pour forth unpremeditated Irish verses. Oliver early became, and through life continued to be, a passionate ad-mirer of the Irish music, and especially of the compositions of Carolan, some of the last notes of whose harp he heard. It ought to be added that Oliver, though by birth one of the Englishry, and though connected by numerous ties with the Established Church, never showed the least sign of that con-temptuous antipathy with which in his days the ruling mi-nority in Ireland too generally regarded the subject majority. So far indeed was he from sharing in the opinions and feel-ings of the caste to which he belonged that he conceived an aversion to the Glorious and Immortal Memory, and, even when George the Third was on the throne, maintained that nothing but the restoration of the banished dynasty could save the country.

From the humble academy kept by the old soldier Goldsmith was removed in his ninth year. He went to several grammar-schools, and acquired some knowledge of the ancient languages. His life at this time seems to have been far from happy. He had, as appears from the admirable portrait of him at Knowle, features harsh even to ugliness. The smallpox had set its mark upon him with more than usual severity. His stature was small, and his limbs ill put together. Among boys little tenderness is shown to personal defects ; and the ridicule excited by poor Oliver's appearance was heightened by a peculiar simplicity and a disposition to blunder which he retained to the last. He became the common butt of boys and masters, was pointed at as a fright in the playground, and flogged as a dunce in the school-room. When he had risen to eminence, those who once derided him ransacked their memory for the events of his early years, and recited repartees and couplets which had dropped from him, and which, though little noticed at the time, were supposed, a quarter of a century later, to indicate the powers which produced *The Vicar of Wakefield* and *The Deserted Village.*

In his seventeenth year Oliver went up to Trinity College, Dublin, as a sizar. The sizars paid nothing for food and tuition, and very little for lodging ; but they had to perform some menial services, from which they have long been relieved. They swept the court; they carried up the dinner to the fellows' table, and changed the plates and poured out the ale of the rulers of the society. Goldsmith was quartered not alone, in a garret, on the window of which his name, scrawled by himself, is still read with interest. From such garrets many men of less parts than his have made their way to the woolsack or to the episcopal bench. But Goldsmith, while he suffered all the humiliations, threw away all the advantages of his situation. He neglected the studies of the place, stood low at the examinations, was turned down to the bottom of his class for playing the buffoon in the lecture-room, was severely reprimanded for pumping on a constable, and was caned by a brutal tutor for giving a ball in the attic story of the college to some gay youths and damsels from the city.

While Oliver was leading at Dublin a life divided between squalid distress and squalid dissipation, his father died, leaving a mere pittance. The youth obtained his bachelor's degree, and left the university. During some time the humble dwelling to which his widowed mother had retired was his home. He was now in his twenty-first year; it was necessary that he should do something; and his education seemed to have fitted him to do nothing but to dress himself in gaudy colours, of which he was as fond as a magpie, to take a hand at cards, to sing Irish airs, to play the flute, to angle in summer, and to tell ghost stories by the fire in winter. He tried five or six professions in turn without success. He applied for ordination; but, as he applied in scarlet clothes, he was speedily turned out of the episcopal palace. He then became tutor in an opulent family, but soon quitted his situation in consequence of a dispute about play. Then he determined to emigrate to America. His relations, with much satisfaction, saw him set out for Cork on a good horse, with thirty pounds

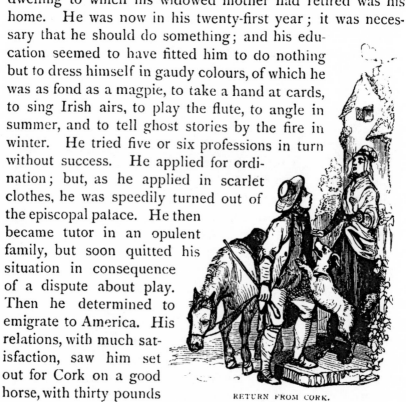

RETURN FROM CORK.

in his pocket. But in six weeks he came back on a miserable hack without a penny, and informed his mother that the ship in which he had taken his passage, having got a fair wind while he was at a party of pleasure, had sailed without him. Then he resolved to study the law. A generous kinsman advanced fifty pounds. With this sum Goldsmith went to Dublin, was enticed into a gambling-house, and lost every shilling. He then thought of medicine. A small purse was made up; and in his twenty-fourth year he was sent to Edinburgh. At Edinburgh he passed eighteen months in nominal attendance on lectures, and picked up some superficial information about chemistry and natural history. Thence he went to Leyden, still pretending to study physic. He left that celebrated university—the third university at which he had resided—in his twenty-seventh year, without a degree, with the merest smattering of medical knowledge, and with no property but his clothes and his flute. His flute, however, proved a useful friend. He rambled on foot through Flanders, France, and Switzerland, playing tunes which everywhere set the peasantry dancing, and which often procured for him a supper and a bed. He wandered as far as Italy. His musical performances, indeed, were not to the taste of the Italians; but he contrived to live on the alms which he obtained at the gates of convents. . . .

In 1756 the wanderer landed at Dover, without a shilling, without a friend, and without a calling. He had, indeed, if his own unsupported evidence may be trusted, obtained from the University of Padua a doctor's degree; but this dignity proved utterly useless to him. In England his flute was not in request; there were no convents; and he was forced to have recourse to a series of desperate expedients. He turned strolling player; but his face and figure were ill-suited to the boards even of the humblest theatre. He pounded drugs and ran about London with phials for charitable chemists.

He joined a swarm of beggars, which made its nest in Axe Yard. He was for a time usher of a school, and felt the miseries and humiliations of this situation so keenly that he thought it a promotion to be permitted to earn his bread as a bookseller's hack; but he soon found the new yoke more galling than the old one, and was glad to become an usher again. He obtained a medical appointment in the service of the East India Company; but the appointment was speedily revoked. Why it was revoked we are not told. The subject was one on which he never liked to talk. It is probable that he was incompetent to perform the duties of the place. Then he presented himself at Surgeons' Hall for examination as mate to a naval hospital. Even to so humble a post he was found unequal. By this time the schoolmaster whom he had served for a morsel of food and the third part of a bed was no more. Nothing remained but to return to the lowest drudgery of literature. Goldsmith took a garret in a

IN GREEN ARBOUR COURT.

miserable court, to which he had to climb from the brink of Fleet Ditch by a dizzy ladder of flagstones called Breakneck Steps. The court and the ascent have long disappeared; but old Londoners well remember both. Here, at thirty, the unlucky adventurer sat down to toil like a galley-slave.

In the succeeding six years he sent to the press some things which have survived, and many which have perished. He produced articles for reviews, magazines, and newspapers; children's books, which, bound in gilt paper and adorned with hideous wood-cuts, appeared in the window of the once far-famed shop at the corner of Saint Paul's Churchyard; *An Inquiry into the State of Polite Learning in Europe,* which, though of little or no value, is still reprinted among his works; a *Life of Beau Nash,* which is not reprinted,* though it well deserves to be so; a superficial and incorrect, but very readable, *History of England,* in a series of letters purporting to be addressed by a nobleman to his son; and some very lively and amusing *Sketches of London Society,* in a series of letters purporting to be addressed by a Chinese traveller to his friends. All these works were anonymous; but some of them were well known to be Goldsmith's; and he gradually rose in the estimation of the booksellers for whom he drudged. He was, indeed, emphatically a popular writer. For accurate research or grave disquisition he was not well qualified by nature or by education. He knew nothing accurately: his reading had been desultory; nor had he meditated deeply on what he had read. He had seen much of the world; but he had noticed and retained little more of what he had seen than some grotesque incidents and characters which happened to strike his fancy. But, though his mind was very scantily stored with materials,

---

* The *Life of Nash* has been reprinted at least three times: in Prior's edition (vol. iii. p. 249); in Cunningham's (vol. iv. p. 35); and in the "Globe" edition (p. 513). This last, however, has appeared (1869) since Macaulay wrote the above.

he used what materials he had in such a way as to produce a wonderful effect.   There have been many greater writers; but perhaps no writer was ever more uniformly agreeable. His style was always pure and easy, and on proper occasions pointed and energetic.   His narratives were always amusing, his descriptions always grotesque, his humour rich and joyous, yet not without an occasional tinge of amiable sadness. About everything that he wrote, serious or sportive, there was a certain natural grace and decorum, hardly to be expected from a man a great part of whose life had been passed among thieves and beggars, street-walkers and merry-andrews, in those squalid dens which are the reproach of great capitals.

As his name gradually became known, the circle of his acquaintance widened.   He was introduced to Johnson, who was then considered as the first of living English writers ; to Reynolds, the first of English painters ; and to Burke, who had not yet entered Parliament, but had distinguished himself greatly by his writings and by the eloquence of his conversation.   With these eminent men Goldsmith became intimate.   In 1763 he was one of the nine original members of that celebrated fraternity which has sometimes been called the Literary Club, but which has always disclaimed that epithet, and still glories in the simple name of The Club.

By this time Goldsmith had quitted his miserable dwelling at the top of Breakneck Steps, and had taken chambers in the more civilized region of the Inns of Court.   But he was still often reduced to pitiable shifts.   Towards the close of 1764 his rent was so long in arrear that his landlady one morning called in the help of a sheriff's officer.   The debtor, in great perplexity, despatched a messenger to Johnson; and Johnson, always friendly, though often surly, sent back the messenger with a guinea, and promised to follow speedily. He came, and found that Goldsmith had changed the guinea, and was railing at the landlady over a bottle of Madeira. Johnson put the cork into the bottle, and entreated his friend

to consider calmly how money was to be procured. Gold-
smith said that he had a novel ready for the press. Johnson
glanced at the manuscript, saw that there were good things

JOHNSON READING "THE VICAR OF WAKEFIELD.'

in it, took it to a bookseller, sold it for £60, and soon return-
ed with the money. The rent was paid, and the sheriff's
officer withdrew. According to one story, Goldsmith gave
his landlady a sharp reprimand for her treatment of him ;
according to another, he insisted on her joining him in a
bowl of punch. Both stories are probably true. The novel
which was thus ushered into the world was *The Vicar of
Wakefield.*

But before *The Vicar of Wakefield* appeared in print came
the great crisis of Goldsmith's literary life. In Christmas
week, 1764, he published a poem, entitled *The Traveller.* It

was the first work to which he had put his name ; and it at once raised him to the rank of a legitimate English classic. The opinion of the most skilful critics was that nothing finer had appeared in verse since the fourth book of *The Dunciad.* In one respect *The Traveller* differs from all Goldsmith's other writings. In general his designs were bad, and his execution good. In *The Traveller* the execution, though deserving of much praise, is far inferior to the design. No philosophical poem, ancient or modern, has a plan so noble, and at the same time so simple. An English wanderer, seated on a crag among the Alps, near the point where three great countries meet, looks down on the boundless prospect, reviews his long pilgrimage, recalls the varieties of scenery, of climate, of government, of religion, of national character, which he has observed, and comes to the conclusion, just or unjust, that our happiness depends little on political institutions, and much on the temper and regulation of our minds.

While the fourth edition of *The Traveller* was on the counters of the booksellers, *The Vicar of Wakefield* appeared, and rapidly obtained a popularity which has lasted down to our own time, and which is likely to last as long as our language. . . .

The success which had attended Goldsmith as a novelist emboldened him to try his fortune as a dramatist. He wrote *The Good-Natured Man*—a piece which had a worse fate than it deserved. Garrick refused to produce it at Drury Lane. It was acted at Covent Garden in 1768, but was coldly received. The author, however, cleared by his benefit nights, and by the sale of the copyright, not less than £500—five times as much as he had made by *The Traveller* and *The Vicar of Wakefield.* The plot of *The Good-Natured Man* is, like almost all Goldsmith's plots, very ill-constructed. But some passages are exquisitely ludicrous; much more ludicrous, indeed, than suited the taste of the town at that time. A canting, mawkish play, entitled *False Delicacy*, had just had an immense run. Sentimentality was all the mode. During some years, more tears were shed at comedies than at tragedies; and a pleasantry which moved the audience to any thing more than a grave smile was reprobated as low. It is not strange, therefore, that the very best scene in *The Good-Natured Man*, that in which Miss Richland finds her lover attended by the bailiff and the bailiff's follower in full court-dresses, should have been mercilessly hissed, and should have been omitted after the first night.

In 1770 appeared *The Deserted Village.* In mere diction and versification this celebrated poem is fully equal, perhaps superior, to *The Traveller*, and it is generally preferred to *The Traveller* by that large class of readers who think, with Bayes in *The Rehearsal*, that the only use of a plan is to bring in fine things. More discerning judges, however, while they admire the beauty of the details, are shocked by one unpardonable fault which pervades the whole. . . . It is made up of incongruous parts. The village in its happy days is a true English village. The village in its decay is an Irish village. The felicity and the misery which Goldsmith has brought close together belong to two different countries, and to two different stages in the progress of society. He had assuredly never seen in his native island such a rural paradise, such a seat of plenty, content, and tranquillity, as his Auburn. He had assuredly never seen in England all the inhabitants of such a paradise turned out of their homes in one day and forced to emigrate in a body to America. The hamlet he had probably seen in Kent; the ejectment he had probably seen in Munster; but by joining the two he has produced something which never was and never will be seen in any part of the world.

In 1773 Goldsmith tried his chance at Covent Garden with a second play, *She Stoops to Conquer.* The manager was not without great difficulty induced to bring this piece out. The sentimental comedy still reigned, and Goldsmith's comedies were not sentimental. *The Good-Natured Man* had been too funny to succeed; yet the mirth of *The Good-Natured Man* was sober when compared with the rich drollery of *She Stoops to Conquer*, which is, in truth, an incomparable farce in five acts. On this occasion, however, genius triumphed. Pit, boxes, and galleries were in a constant roar of laughter. If any bigoted admirer of Kelly and Cumberland ventured to hiss or groan, he was speedily silenced by a general cry of "Turn him out," or "Throw him over." Two generations have since confirmed the verdict which was pronounced on that night.

While Goldsmith was writing *The Deserted Village* and *She Stoops to Conquer*, he was employed on works of a very different kind—works from which he derived little reputation but much profit. He compiled for the use of schools a *History of Rome*, by which he made £300; a *History of England*, by which he made £600; a *History of Greece*, for which he received £250; a *Natural History*, for which the booksellers covenanted to pay him 800 guineas. These works he produced without any elaborate research, by merely selecting, abridging, and translating into his own clear, pure, and flowing language what he found in books well known to the world, but too bulky or too dry for boys and girls. He committed some strange blunders; for he knew nothing with accuracy. Thus in his *History of England* he tells us that Naseby is in Yorkshire; nor did he correct this mistake when the book was reprinted. He was very nearly hoaxed into putting into *The History of Greece* an account of a battle between Alexander the Great and Montezuma. In his *Animated Nature* he relates, with faith and with perfect gravity, all the most absurd lies which he could find in books of travels about gigantic Patagonians, monkeys that preach sermons, nightingales that repeat long conversations. "If he can tell a horse from a cow," says Johnson, "that is the extent of his knowledge of zoology." How little Goldsmith

was qualified to write about the physical sciences is suffi-
ciently proved by two anecdotes. He on one occasion de-
nied that the sun is longer in the northern than in the south-
ern signs. It was vain to cite the authority of Maupertuis.
"Maupertuis !" he cried, " I understand those matters better
than Maupertuis." On another occasion he, in defiance of
the evidence of his own senses, maintained obstinately, and
even angrily, that he chewed his dinner by moving his upper
jaw.

Yet, ignorant as Goldsmith was, few writers have done
more to make the first steps in the laborious road to knowl-
edge easy and pleasant. His compilations are widely dis-
tinguished from the compilations of ordinary book-makers.
He was a great, perhaps an unequalled, master of the arts of
selection and condensation. In these respects his histories
of Rome and of England, and still more his own abridg-
ments of these histories, well deserve to be studied. In
general nothing is less attractive than an epitome; but the
epitomes of Goldsmith, even when most concise, are always
amusing; and to read them is considered by intelligent chil-
dren not as a task but as a pleasure.

Goldsmith might now be considered as a prosperous man.
He had the means of living in comfort, and even in what to
one who had so often slept in barns and on bulks must have
been luxury. His fame was great and was constantly ris-
ing. He lived in what was intellectually far the best soci-
ety of the kingdom—in a society in which no talent or ac-
complishment was wanting, and in which the art of conver-
sation was cultivated with splendid success. There prob-
ably were never four talkers more admirable in four differ-
ent ways than Johnson, Burke, Beauclerk, and Garrick; and
Goldsmith was on terms of intimacy with all the four. He
aspired to share in their colloquial renown ; but never was
ambition more unfortunate. It may seem strange that a
man who wrote with so much perspicuity, vivacity, and grace

should have been, whenever he took a part in conversation, an empty, noisy, blundering rattle. But on this point the evidence is overwhelming. So extraordinary was the contrast between Goldsmith's published works and the silly things which he said, that Horace Walpole described him as an inspired idiot. "Noll," said Garrick, "wrote like an angel, and talked like poor Pol." Chamier declared that it was a hard exercise of faith to believe that so foolish a chatterer could have really written *The Traveller.* Even Boswell could say, with contemptuous compassion, that he liked very well to hear honest Goldsmith run on. "Yes, sir," said Johnson, "but he should not like to hear himself." Minds differ as rivers differ. There are transparent and sparkling rivers from which it is delightful to drink as they flow; to such rivers the minds of such men as Burke and Johnson may be compared. But there are rivers of which the water when first drawn is turbid and noisome, but becomes pellucid as crystal and delicious to the taste if it be suffered to stand till it has deposited a sediment; and such a river is a type of the mind of Goldsmith. His first thoughts on every subject were confused even to absurdity, but they required only a little time to work themselves clear. When he wrote they had that time, and therefore his readers pronounced him a man of genius ; but when he talked he talked nonsense, and made himself the laughing-stock of his hearers. He was painfully sensible of his inferiority in conversation ; he felt every failure keenly ; yet he had not sufficient judgment and self-command to hold his tongue. His animal spirits and vanity were always impelling him to try to do the one thing which he could not do. After every attempt he felt that he had exposed himself, and writhed with shame and vexation; yet the next moment he began again.

His associates seem to have regarded him with kindness, which, in spite of their admiration of his writings, was not unmixed with contempt. In truth, there was in his character much to love, but very little to respect. His heart was soft, even to weakness; he was so generous that he quite forgot to be just; he forgave injuries so readily that he might be said to invite them; and was so liberal to beggars that he had nothing left for his tailor and his butcher. He was vain, sensual, frivolous, profuse, improvident. One vice of a darker shade was imputed to him—envy. But there is not the least reason to believe that this bad passion, though it sometimes made him wince and utter fretful exclamations, ever impelled him to injure by wicked arts the reputation of any of his rivals. The truth probably is that he was not more envious, but merely less prudent than his neighbours. His heart was on his lips. All those small jealousies which are but too common among men of letters, but which a man of letters who is also a man of the world does his best to conceal, Goldsmith avowed with the simplicity of a child. . . . He was neither ill-natured enough nor long-headed enough to be guilty of any malicious act which required contrivance and disguise.

Goldsmith has sometimes been represented as a man of genius, cruelly treated by the world, and doomed to struggle with difficulties which at last broke his heart. But no representation can be more remote from the truth. He did, indeed, go through much sharp misery before he had done any thing considerable in literature. But after his name had appeared on the title-page of *The Traveller*, he had none but himself to blame for his distresses. His average income during the last seven years of his life certainly exceeded £400 a year, and £400 a year ranked among the incomes of that day at least as high as £800 a year would rank at present. A single man living in the Temple with £400 a year might then be called opulent. Not one in ten of the young gentlemen of good families who were studying the law there had so much. But all the wealth which Lord Clive had brought from Bengal and Sir Lawrence Dundas from Germany joined together would not have sufficed for Goldsmith. He spent twice as much as he had. He wore fine clothes, gave dinners of several courses, paid court to venal beauties. He had also, it should be remembered to the honour of his heart, though not of his head, a guinea, or five, or ten, according to the state of his purse, ready for any tale of distress, true or false. But it was not in dress or feasting, in promiscuous amours or promiscuous charities, that his chief expense lay. He had been from boyhood a gambler, and at once the most sanguine and the most unskilful of gamblers.* For a time he put off the day of inevitable ruin by temporary expedients. He obtained advances from booksellers by promising to execute works which he never began. But at length this source of supply failed. He owed more than £2000, and he saw no hope of extrication from his embarrassments. His spirits and health gave way. He was attacked by a nervous fever, which he thought himself competent to treat. It would have been happy for him if his medical skill had been appreciated as justly by himself as by others. Notwithstanding the degree which he pretended to have received at Padua, he could procure no patients. "I do not practice," he once said; "I make it a rule to prescribe only for my friends." "Pray, dear Doctor," said Beauclerk, "alter your rule, and prescribe only for your enemies." Goldsmith now, in spite of this excellent advice, prescribed for himself. The remedy aggravated the malady. The sick man was induced to call in real physicians, and they at one time imagined that they had cured the disease. Still his weakness and restlessness continued. He could get no sleep; he could take no food. "You are worse," said one of his medical attendants, "than you should be from the degree of fever which you have. Is your mind at ease?" "No, it is not," were the last recorded words of Oliver Goldsmith. He died on the 3d of April, 1774, in his

* See extract from Irving, p. 140.

forty-sixth year. He was laid in the churchyard of the Temple ; but the spot was not marked by any inscription, and is now forgotten. The coffin was followed by Burke and Reynolds. Both these great men were sincere mourners. Burke, when he heard of Goldsmith's death, had burst into a flood of tears. Reynolds had been so much moved by the news that he had flung aside his brush and pallet for the day.

A short time after Goldsmith's death a little poem appeared, which will, as long as our language lasts, associate the names of his two illustrious friends with his own. It has already been mentioned that he sometimes felt keenly the sarcasm which his wild, blundering talk brought upon him. He was, not long before his last illness, provoked into retaliating. He wisely betook himself to his pen, and at that weapon he proved himself a match for all his assailants together. Within a small compass he drew with a singularly easy and vigorous pencil the characters of nine or ten of his intimate associates. Though this little work did not receive his last touches, it must always be regarded as a masterpiece. It is impossible, however, not to wish that four or five likenesses which have no interest for posterity were wanting to that noble gallery, and that their places were supplied by sketches of Johnson and Gibbon, as happy and vivid as the sketches of Burke and Garrick.

Some of Goldsmith's friends and admirers honoured him with a cenotaph in Westminster Abbey. Nollekens was the sculptor, and Johnson wrote the inscription. It is much to be lamented that Johnson did not leave to posterity a more durable and a more valuable memorial of his friend. A life of Goldsmith would have been an inestimable addition to the *Lives of the Poets.* No man appreciated Goldsmith's writings more justly than Johnson; no man was better acquainted with Goldsmith's character and habits ; and no man was more competent to delineate with truth and spirit the peculiarities of a mind in which great powers were found in company with great weaknesses. But the list of poets to whose works Johnson was requested by the booksellers to furnish prefaces ended with Lyttleton, who died in 1773. The line seems to have been drawn expressly for the purpose of excluding the person whose portrait would have most fitly closed the series. Goldsmith, however, has been fortunate in his biographers. Within a few years his life has been written by Mr. Prior, by Mr. Washington Irving, and by Mr. Forster. The diligence of Mr. Prior deserves great praise; the style of Mr. Washington Irving is always pleasing; but the highest place must in justice be assigned to the eminently interesting work of Mr. Forster.

OLIVARII GOLDSMITH | Hoc monumento memoriam coluit
Poetæ, Physici, Historici, | Sodalium amor,

GOLDSMITH'S MONUMENT IN WESTMINSTER ABBEY.

The Tablet is over the south door in Poets' Corner, between the

monuments of Gay and the Duke of Argyll. The Latin inscription
(in which the year of the poet's birth is wrongly given) is as follows:

OLIVARII GOLDSMITH,

Poetæ, Physici, Historici,

Qui nullum fere scribendi genus

Non tetigit,

Nullum quod tetigit non ornavit:

Sive risus essent movendi,

Sive lacrymæ,

Affectuum potens at lenis dominator:

Ingenio sublimis, vividus, versatilis,

Oratione grandis, nitidus, venustus:

Hoc monumento memoriam coluit

Sodalium amor,

Amicorum fides,

Lectorum veneratio.

Natus in Hibernia, Forniæ Longfordiensis

In loco cui nomen Pallas,

Nov. xxix. MDCCXXXI.

Eblanæ literis institutus;

Obiit Londini,

Apr. iv. MDCCLXXIV.

— — —

OF OLIVER GOLDSMITH—

Poet, Naturalist, Historian,

Who left scarcely any kind of writing

Untouched,

And touched nothing that he did not adorn:

Whether smiles were to be stirred

Or tears,

Commanding our emotions, yet a gentle master:

In genius lofty, lively, versatile,

In style weighty, clear, engaging—

The memory in this monument is cherished

By the love of Companions,

The faithfulness of Friends,

The reverence of Readers.

He was born in Ireland,

At a place called Pallas,

[In the parish] of Forney, [and county] of Longford,

On Nov. 29th, 1731.

Trained in letters at Dublin.

Died in London,

April 4th, 1774.

HOGARTH'S PORTRAIT OF GOLDSMITH.

SELECTIONS FROM OTHER MEMOIRS OF GOLDSMITH.

FROM THACKERAY'S "ENGLISH HUMOURISTS." *

Who of the millions whom he has amused does not love him? To be the most beloved of English writers, what a title that is for a man !† A wild youth, wayward but full of

* *The English Humourists of the Eighteenth Century.* A Series of Lectures. By W. M. Thackeray. Harper's edition, p. 248 foll.

† " He was a friend to virtue, and in his most playful pages never forgets what is due to it. A gentleness, delicacy, and purity of feeling distinguishes whatever he wrote, and bears a correspondence to the generosity of a disposition which knew no bounds but his last guinea. . . .

" The admirable ease and grace of the narrative, as well as the pleasing truth with which the principal characters are designed, make *The Vicar of Wakefield* one of the most delicious morsels of fictitious composition on which the human mind was ever employed. . . .

" We read *The Vicar of Wakefield* in youth and in age ; we return to it again and again, and bless the memory of an author who contrives so well to reconcile us to human nature."—SIR WALTER SCOTT.

tenderness and affection, quits the country village where his boyhood has been passed in happy musing, in idle shelter, in fond longing to see the great world out of doors, and achieve name and fortune; and after years of dire struggle, and neglect and poverty, his heart turning back as fondly to his native place as it had longed eagerly for change when sheltered there, he writes a book and a poem, full of the recollections and feelings of home—he paints the friends and scenes of his youth, and peoples Auburn and Wakefield with remembrances of Lissoy. Wander he must, but he carries away a home-relic with him, and dies with it on his breast. His nature is truant; in repose it longs for change: as on the journey it looks back for friends and quiet. He passes to-day in building an air-castle for to-morrow, or in writing yesterday's elegy; and he would fly away this hour, but that a cage necessity keeps him. What is the charm of his verse, of his style and humour? His sweet regrets, his delicate compassion, his soft smile, his tremulous sympathy, the weakness which he owns? Your love for him is half pity. You come hot and tired from the day's battle, and this sweet minstrel sings to you. Who could harm the kind vagrant harper? Whom did he ever hurt? He carries no weapon— save the harp on which he plays to you; and with which he delights great and humble, young and old, the captains in the tents or the soldiers round the fire, or the women and children in the villages, at whose porches he stops and sings his simple songs of love and beauty. With that sweet story of *The Vicar of Wakefield* he has found entry into every castle and every hamlet in Europe. Not one of us, however busy or hard, but once or twice in our lives has passed an evening with him, and undergone the charm of his delightful music. . . .

The small-pox, which scourged all Europe at that time, and ravaged the roses off the cheeks of half the world, fell foul of poor little Oliver's face when the child was eight years old, and left him scarred and disfigured for his life. An old woman in his father's village taught him his letters, and pronounced him a dunce. Paddy Byrne, the hedge-schoolmaster, took him in hand; and from Paddy Byrne he was transmitted to a clergyman at Elphin. When a child was sent to school in those days, the classic phrase was that he was placed under Mr. So-and-So's *ferule*. Poor little ancestors! It is hard to think how ruthlessly you were birched; and how much of needless whipping and tears our small forefathers had to undergo! A relative, kind Uncle Contarine, took the main charge of little Noll, who went through his school-days righteously, doing as little work as he could; robbing orchards, playing at ball, and making his pocket-money fly about whenever fortune sent it to him. Everybody knows the story of that famous "Mistake of a Night," when the young school-boy, provided with a guinea and a nag, rode up to the "best house" in Ardagh, called for the landlord's company over a bottle of wine at supper, and for a hot cake for breakfast in the morning, and found when he asked for the bill that the best house was Squire Featherstone's, and not the inn for which he mistook it. Who does not know every story about Goldsmith? That is a delightful and fantastic picture of the child dancing and capering about in the kitchen at home, when the old fiddler gibed at him for his ugliness—and called him Æsop, and little Noll made his repartee of "Heralds proclaim aloud this saying—see Æsop dancing and his monkey playing." One can fancy the queer, pitiful look of humour and appeal from that little scarred face—the funny little dancing figure, the funny little brogue. In his life, and his writings, which are the honest expression of it, he is constantly bewailing that homely face and person; anon he surveys them in the glass ruefully, and presently assumes the most comical dignity. . . .

I spoke in a former lecture of that high courage which

enabled Fielding, in spite of disease, remorse, and poverty, always to retain a cheerful spirit and to keep his manly benevolence and love of truth intact, as if these treasures had been confided to him for the public benefit, and he was accountable to posterity for their honourable employ; and a constancy equally happy and admirable I think was shown by Goldsmith, whose sweet and friendly nature bloomed kindly always in the midst of a life's storm and rain and bitter weather.* The poor fellow was never so friendless but he could befriend some one; never so pinched and

NIGHT WANDERINGS.

* "An 'inspired idiot,' Goldsmith, hangs strangely about him [John-son]. . . . Yet, on the whole, there is no evil in the 'gooseberry-fool,' but rather much good; of a finer, if of a weaker sort than Johnson's; and all the more genuine that he himself could never become *conscious* of it—though, unhappily, never cease *attempting* to become so: the author

wretched but he could give of his crust and speak his word of compassion. If he had but his flute left, he could give that, and make the children happy in the dreary London court. He could give the coals in that queer coal-scuttle we read of to his poor neighbour; he could give away his blankets in college to the poor widow, and warm himself as he best might in the feathers; he could pawn his coat to save his landlord from jail; when he was a school-usher, he spent his earnings in treats for the boys, and the good-natured schoolmaster's wife said justly that she ought to keep Mr. Goldsmith's money as well as the young gentlemen's. When he met his pupils in later life, nothing would satisfy the Doctor but he must treat them still. "Have you seen the print of me after Sir Joshua Reynolds?" he asked of one of his old pupils. "Not seen it? not bought it? Sure, Jack, if your picture had been published, I'd not have been without it half an hour." His purse and his heart were everybody's, and his friends' as much as his own. When he was at the height of his reputation, and the Earl of Northumberland, going as Lord Lieutenant to Ireland, asked if he could be of any service to Dr. Goldsmith, Goldsmith recommended his brother, and not himself, to the great man. "My patrons," he gallantly said, "are the booksellers, and I want no others." Hard patrons they were, and hard work he did; but he did not complain much. If in his early writings some bitter words escaped him, some allusions to neglect and poverty, he withdrew these expressions when his works were republished, and better days seemed to open for him; and he did not care to complain that printer or publisher had overlooked his merit or left him poor. The Court face was turned from honest Oliver—the Court patronized Beattie; the fashion did not shine on him—fashion adored Sterne.

of the genuine *Vicar of Wakefield*, nill he will he, must needs fly towards such a mass of genuine manhood."—CARLYLE's *Essays* (second edition), vol. iv. p. 91.

Fashion pronounced Kelly to be the great writer of comedy of his day. A little—not ill-humour, but plaintiveness— a little betrayal of wounded pride which he showed render him not the less amiable. The author of *The Vicar of Wakefield* had a right to protest when Newbery kept back the MS. for two years; had a right to be a little peevish with Sterne; a little angry when Coleman's actors declined their parts in his delightful comedy, when the manager refused to have a scene painted for it, and pronounced its damnation before hearing. He had not the great public with him; but he had the noble Johnson, and the admirable Reynolds,

DR. SAMUEL JOHNSON.—[FROM A PAINTING BY SIR JOSHUA REYNOLDS, 1778]

and the great Gibbon, and the great Burke, and the great Fox—friends and admirers illustrious indeed, as famous as those who, fifty years before, sat round Pope's table.

C

Nobody knows, and I dare say Goldsmith's buoyant temper kept no account of all the pains which he endured during the early period of his literary career. Should any man of letters in our day have to bear up against such, Heaven grant he may come out of the period of misfortune with such a pure, kind heart as that which Goldsmith obstinately bore in his breast. The insults to which he had to submit are shocking to read of—slander, contumely, vulgar satire, brutal malignity perverting his commonest motives and actions: he had his share of these, and one's anger is roused at reading of them, as it is at seeing a woman insulted or a child assaulted, at the notion that a creature so very gentle and weak and full of love should have had to suffer so. And he had worse than insult to undergo—to own to fault, and deprecate the anger of ruffians. There is a letter of his extant to one Griffiths, a bookseller, in which poor Goldsmith is forced to confess that certain books sent by Griffiths are in the hands of a friend from whom Goldsmith had been forced to borrow money. "He was wild, sir," Johnson said, speaking of Goldsmith to Boswell, with his great, wise benevolence and noble mercifulness of heart—"Dr. Goldsmith was wild, sir; but he is so no more." Ah! if we pity the good and weak man who suffers undeservedly, let us deal very gently with him from whom misery extorts not only tears, but shame; let us think humbly and charitably of the human nature that suffers so sadly and falls so low. Whose turn may it be to-morrow? What weak heart, confident before trial, may not succumb under temptation invincible? Cover the good man who has been vanquished—cover his face and pass on. . . .

Think of him reckless, thriftless, vain if you like; but merciful, gentle, generous, full of love and pity. He passes out of our life, and goes to render his account beyond it. Think of the poor pensioners weeping at his grave; think of the noble spirits that admired and deplored him; think of the righteous pen that wrote his epitaph—and of the wonderful and unanimous response of affection with which the world has paid back the love he gave it. His humour delighting us still; his song fresh and beautiful as when first he charmed with it; his words in all our mouths; his very weaknesses beloved and familiar—his benevolent spirit seems still to smile upon us; to do gentle kindnesses; to succour with sweet charity; to soothe, caress, and forgive; to plead with the fortunate for the unhappy and the poor.

FROM "RANDOM RECOLLECTIONS," BY GEORGE COLMAN THE YOUNGER.*

I was only five years old when Goldsmith took me on his knee, while he was drinking coffee one evening with my father, and began to play with me, which amiable act I returned with the ingratitude of a peevish brat by giving him a very smart slap in the face; it must have been a tingler, for it left the marks of my little spiteful paw upon his cheek. This infantile outrage was followed by summary justice, and I was locked up by my indignant father in an adjoining room to undergo solitary imprisonment in the dark. Here I began to howl and scream most abominably. . . . At length a generous friend appeared to extricate me from jeopardy ; . . . it was the tender-hearted Doctor himself, with a lighted candle in his hand, and a smile upon his countenance, which was still partially red from the effects of my petulance. I sulked and sobbed, and he fondled and soothed until I began to brighten. Goldsmith, who in regard to children was like the Village Preacher he has so beautifully described—for

"Their welfare pleas'd him, and their cares distress'd"—

seized the propitious moment of returning good-humour; so he put down the candle and began to conjure. He placed

* Vol. i. p. 63.

three hats which happened to be in the room upon the car-
pet, and a shilling under each; the shillings, he told me, were
England, France, and Spain. "Hey, presto, cockolorum!"
cried the Doctor; and, lo! on uncovering the shillings, which
had been dispersed, each beneath a separate hat, they were
all found congregated under one. I was no politician at five
years old, and therefore might not have wondered at the
sudden revolution which brought England, France, and Spain
all under one crown; but, as I was also no conjurer, it
amazed me beyond measure. . . . From that time, whenever
the Doctor came to visit my father,

> "I pluck'd his gown to share the good man's smile;"

a game of romps constantly ensued, and we were always cor-
dial friends and merry playfellows. Our unequal companion-
ship varied somewhat in point of sports as I grew older, but
it did not last long; my senior playmate died, alas! in his
forty-fifth year, some months after I had attained my eleventh.
His death, it has been thought, was hastened by "mental in-
quietude." If this supposition be true, never did the tur-
moils of life subdue a mind more warm with sympathy for
the misfortunes of our fellow-creatures. But his character is
familiar to every one who reads. In all the numerous ac-
counts of his virtues and foibles, his genius and absurdities,
his knowledge of nature and his ignorance of the world, his
"compassion for another's woe" was always predominant;
and my trivial story of his humouring a froward child weighs
but a feather in the recorded scale of his benevolence.

FROM CAMPBELL'S "BRITISH POETS."*

Goldsmith's poetry enjoys a calm and steady popularity.
It inspires us, indeed, with no admiration of daring design
or of fertile invention; but it presents, within its narrow

* *Specimens of the British Poets,* Cunningham's edit., London, 1841.

limits, a distinct and unbroken view of poetical delightful-
ness. His descriptions and sentiments have the pure zest
of nature. He is refined without false delicacy, and correct
without insipidity. Perhaps there is an intellectual com-
posure in his manner, which may in some passages be said
to approach to the reserved and prosaic; but he unbends
from this graver strain of reflection to tenderness, and even
to playfulness, with an ease and grace almost exclusively his
own, and connects extensive views of the happiness and in-
terests of society with pictures of life that touch the heart
by their familiarity. His language is certainly simple,
though it is not cast in a rugged or careless mould. He is
no disciple of the gaunt and famished school of simplicity.
Deliberately as he wrote, he can not be accused of wanting
natural and idiomatic expression; but still it is select and
refined expression. He uses the ornaments which must
always distinguish true poetry from prose; and when he
adopts colloquial plainness, it is with the utmost care and
skill to avoid a vulgar humility. There is more of this sus-
tained simplicity, of this chaste economy and choice of
words, in Goldsmith than in any modern poet, or perhaps
than would be attainable or desirable as a standard for
every writer of rhyme. In extensive narrative poems such
a style would be too difficult. There is a noble propriety
even in the careless strength of great poems, as in the rough-
ness of castle walls; and, generally speaking, where there is
a long course of story or observation of life to be pursued,
such exquisite touches as those of Goldsmith would be too
costly materials for sustaining it. But let us not imagine
that the serene graces of this poet were not admirably
adapted to his subjects. His poetry is not that of impetu-
ous, but of contemplative sensibility; of a spirit breathing
its regrets and recollections in a tone that has no disso-
nance with the calm of philosophical reflection. He takes
rather elevated speculative views of the causes of good and

evil in society; at the same time the objects which are most endeared to his imagination are those of familiar and simple interest; and the domestic affections may be said to be the only genii of his romance. The tendency towards abstracted observation in his poetry agrees peculiarly with the compendious form of expression which he studied;* while the home-felt joys, on which his fancy loved to repose, required at once the chastest and sweetest colours of language to make them harmonize with the dignity of a philosophical poem. His whole manner has a still depth of feeling and reflection, which gives back the image of nature unruffled and minutely. He has no redundant thoughts or false transports ; but seems on every occasion to have weighed the impulse to which he surrendered himself. Whatever ardour or casual felicities he may have thus sacrificed, he gained a high degree of purity and self-possession. His chaste pathos makes him an insinuating moralist, and throws a charm of Claude-like softness over his descriptions of homely objects that would seem only fit to be the subjects of Dutch painting. But his quiet enthusiasm leads the affections to humble things without a vulgar association; and he inspires us with a fondness to trace the simplest recollections of Auburn, till we count the furniture of its alehouse and listen to

"The varnish'd clock that click'd behind the door."

He betrays so little effort to make us visionary by the usual and palpable fictions of his art; he keeps apparently so close to realities, and draws certain conclusions respecting the radical interests of man so boldly and decidedly,

* There is perhaps no couplet in English rhyme more perspicuously condensed than those two lines of *The Traveller* in which he describes the once flattering, vain, and happy character of the French :

"They please, are pleas'd, they give to get esteem,
Till, seeming blest, they grow to what they seem."

that we pay him a compliment, not always extended to the tuneful tribe—that of judging his sentiments by their strict and logical interpretation. In thus judging him by the test of his philosophical spirit, I am not prepared to say that he is a purely impartial theorist. He advances general positions respecting the happiness of society, founded on limited views of truth, and under the bias of local feelings. He contemplates only one side of the question. It must be always thus in poetry. Let the mind be ever so tranquilly disposed to reflection, yet if it retain poetical sensation, it will embrace only those speculative opinions that fall in with the tone of the imagination. Yet I am not disposed to consider his principles as absurd, or his representations of life as the mere reveries of fancy.

FROM FORSTER'S LIFE OF THE POET.*

Of the many clever and indeed wonderful writings that from age to age are poured forth into the world, what is it that puts upon the few the stamp of immortality, and makes them seem indestructible as nature? What is it but their wise rejection of everything superfluous?—being grave histories, or natural stories, of everything that is *not* history or nature?—being poems, of everything that is *not* poetry, however much it may resemble it; and especially of that prodigal accumulation of thoughts and images which, till properly sifted and selected, is as the unhewn to the chiselled marble? What is it, in short, but that unity, completeness, polish, and perfectness in every part which Goldsmith attained? It may be said that his range is limited, and that, whether in his poetry or his prose, he seldom wanders far from the ground of his own experience; but within that circle how potent is his magic, what a command it exercises over the happiest forms of art, with what a versatile grace it moves

* *Life and Times of Oliver Goldsmith,* by John Forster, vol. i. p. 228.

between what saddens us in humour or smiles on us in grief, and how unerring our response of laughter or of tears ! Thus, his pictures may be small; may be far from historical pieces, amazing or confounding us ; may be even, if severest criticism will have it so, mere happy *tableaux de genre* hanging up against our walls; but their colours are exquisite and unfading ; they have that universal expression which never rises higher than the comprehension of the humblest, yet is ever on a level with the understanding and appreciation of the loftiest ; they possess that familiar sweetness of household expression which wins them welcome, alike where the rich inhabit and in huts where poor men lie ; and there, improving and gladdening all, they are likely to hang forever.

FROM IRVING'S LIFE OF THE POET.[*]

There are few writers for whom the reader feels such personal kindness as for Oliver Goldsmith, for few have so eminently possessed the magic gift of identifying themselves with their writings. We read his character in every page, and grow into familiar intimacy with him as we read. The artless benevolence that beams throughout his works; the whimsical yet amiable views of human life and human nature; the unforced humour, blending so happily with good-feeling and good-sense, and singularly dashed at times with a pleasing melancholy; even the very nature of his mellow and flowing and softly tinted style—all seem to bespeak his moral as well as his intellectual qualities, and make us love the man at the same time that we admire the author. While the productions of writers of loftier pretension and more sounding names are suffered to moulder on our shelves, those of Goldsmith are cherished and laid in our bosoms. We do not quote them with ostentation, but they mingle

* *Oliver Goldsmith : a Biography.* By Washington Irving. Edit. of 1849, p. 17 foll.

with our minds, sweeten our tempers, and harmonize our thoughts; they put us in good-humour with ourselves and with the world, and in so doing they make us happier and better men.

An acquaintance with the private biography of Goldsmith lets us into the secret of his gifted pages. We there discover them to be little more than transcripts of his own heart and picturings of his fortunes. There he shows himself the same kind, artless, good-humoured, excursive, sensible, whimsical, intelligent being that he appears in his writings. Scarcely an adventure or character is given in his works that may not be traced to his own parti-coloured story. Many of his most ludicrous scenes and ridiculous incidents have been drawn from his own blunders and mischances, and he seems really to have been buffeted into almost every maxim imparted by him for the instruction of his reader. ...

Never was the trite, because sage apothegm, that "The child is father to the man," more fully verified than in the case of Goldsmith. He is shy, awkward, and blundering in childhood, yet full of sensibility; he is a butt for the jeers and jokes of his companions, but apt to surprise and confound them by sudden and witty repartees; he is dull and stupid at his tasks, yet an eager and intelligent devourer of the travelling tales and campaigning stories of his half-military pedagogue; he may be a dunce, but he is already a rhymer; and his early scintillations of poetry awaken the expectations of his friends. He seems from infancy to have been compounded of two natures—one bright, the other blundering; or to have had fairy gifts laid in his cradle by the "good people" who haunted his birthplace, the old goblin mansion on the banks of the Inny.

He carries with him the wayward elfin spirit, if we may so term it, throughout his career. His fairy gifts are of no avail at school, academy, or college : they unfit him for close study and practical science, and render him heedless of

everything that does not address itself to his poetical im-
agination and genial and festive feelings; they dispose him
to break away from restraint, to stroll about hedges, green
lanes, and haunted streams, to revel with jovial companions,
or to rove the country like a gypsy in quest of odd advent-
ures.

As if confiding in these delusive gifts, he takes no heed
of the present nor care for the future, lays no regular and
solid foundation of knowledge, follows out no plan, adopts
and discards those recommended by his friends; at one time
prepares for the ministry, next turns to the law, and then
fixes upon medicine. He repairs to Edinburgh, the great
emporium of medical science, but the fairy gifts accompany
him; he idles and frolics away his time there, imbibing only
such knowledge as is agreeable to him; makes an excursion
to the poetical regions of the Highlands; and having walk-
ed the hospitals for the customary time, sets off to ramble
over the Continent, in quest of novelty rather than knowl-
edge. His whole tour is a poetical one. He fancies he is
playing the philosopher while he is really playing the poet;
and though professedly he attends lectures and visits foreign
universities, so deficient is he on his return, in the studies
for which he set out, that he fails in an examination as a
surgeon's mate ; and while figuring as a doctor of medicine,
is outvied on a point of practice by his apothecary. Baffled
in every regular pursuit, after trying in vain some of the
humbler callings of commonplace life, he is driven almost
by chance to the exercise of his pen, and here the fairy gifts
come to his assistance. For a long time, however, he seems
unaware of the magic properties of that pen : he uses it only
as a makeshift until he can find a *legitimate* means of sup-
port. He is not a learned man, and can write but meagrely
and at second-hand on learned subjects; but he has a quick
convertible talent that seizes lightly on the points of knowl-
edge necessary to the illustration of a theme: his writings

for a time are desultory, the fruits of what he has seen and felt, or what he has recently and hastily read; but his gifted pen transmutes everything into gold, and his own genial nature reflects its sunshine through his pages.

Still unaware of his powers, he throws off his writings anonymously, to go with the writings of less favoured men; and it is a long time, and after a bitter struggle with poverty and humiliation, before he acquires confidence in his literary talent as a means of support, and begins to dream of reputation.

From this time his pen is a wand of power in his hand, and he has only to use it discreetly to make it competent to all his wants. But discretion is not a part of Goldsmith's nature; and it seems the property of these fairy gifts to be accompanied by moods and temperaments to render their effect precarious. The heedlessness of his early days; his disposition for social enjoyment; his habit of throwing the present on the neck of the future, still continue. His expenses forerun his means; he incurs debts on the faith of what his magic pen is to produce, and then, under the pressure of his debts, sacrifices its productions for prices far below their value. It is a redeeming circumstance in his prodigality that it is lavished oftener upon others than upon himself: he gives without thought or stint, and is the continual dupe of his benevolence and his trustfulness in human nature. We may say of him as he says of one of his heroes, " He could not stifle the natural impulse which he had to do good, but frequently borrowed money to relieve the distressed; and when he knew not conveniently where to borrow, he has been observed to shed tears as he passed through the wretched suppliants who attended his gate. . . . His simplicity in trusting persons whom he had no previous reasons to place confidence in seems to be one of those lights of his character which, while they impeach his understanding, do honour to his benevolence. The low and the timid are ever suspicious;

but a heart impressed with honourable sentiments expects from others sympathetic sincerity."*

His heedlessness in pecuniary matters, which had render-ed his life a struggle with poverty even in the days of his obscurity, rendered the struggle still more intense when his fairy gifts had elevated him into the society of the wealthy and luxurious, and imposed on his simple and generous spirit fancied obligations to a more ample and bounteous display.

"How comes it," says a recent and ingenious critic, "that in all the miry paths of life which he had trod, no speck ever sullied the robe of his modest and graceful muse. How amid all that love of inferior company, which never to the last forsook him, did he keep his genius so free from every touch of vulgarity?"

We answer that it was owing to the innate purity and goodness of his nature; there was nothing in it that assimi-lated to vice and vulgarity. Though his circumstances often compelled him to associate with the poor, they never could betray him into companionship with the depraved. His rel-ish for humour and for the study of character, as we have before observed, brought him often into convivial company of a vulgar kind; but he discriminated between their vulgar-ity and their amusing qualities, or rather wrought from the whole those familiar pictures of life which form the staple of his most popular writings.

Much, too, of this intact purity of heart may be ascribed to the lessons of his infancy under the paternal roof; to the gentle, benevolent, elevated, unworldly maxims of his father, who, "passing rich with forty pounds a year," infused a spirit into his child which riches could not deprave nor poverty de-grade. Much of his boyhood, too, had been passed in the household of his uncle, the amiable and generous Contarine; where he talked of literature with the good pastor, and prac-ticed music with his daughter, and delighted them both by

* Goldsmith's *Life of Nash.*

his juvenile attempts at poetry. These early associations breathed a grace and refinement into his mind, and tuned it up after the rough sports on the green or the frolics at the tavern. These led him to turn from the roaring glees of the club to listen to the harp of his cousin Jane, and from the rustic triumph of "throwing sledge" to a stroll with his flute along the pastoral banks of the Inny.

The gentle spirit of his father walked with him through life, a pure and virtuous monitor; and in all the vicissitudes of his career, we find him ever more chastened in mind by the sweet and holy recollections of the home of his infancy.

It has been questioned whether he really had any religious feeling. Those who raise the question have never considered well his writings; his *Vicar of Wakefield* and his pictures of the village pastor present religion under its most endearing forms, and with a feeling that could only flow from the deep convictions of the heart. When his fair travelling companions at Paris urged him to read the Church Service on a Sunday, he replied that "he was not worthy to do it." He had seen in early life the sacred offices performed by his father and his brother, with a solemnity which had sanctified them in his memory; how could he presume to undertake such functions? His religion has been called in question by Johnson and by Boswell: he certainly had not the gloomy hypochondriacal piety of the one nor the babbling mouth-piety of the other; but the spirit of Christian charity breathed forth in his writings and illustrated in his conduct give us reason to believe he had the indwelling religion of the soul. . . .

From the general tone of Goldsmith's biography, it is evident that his faults, at the worst, were but negative, while his merits were great and decided. He was no one's enemy but his own; his errors, in the main, inflicted evil on none but himself, and were so blended with humorous and even affecting circumstances as to disarm anger and conciliate kindness. Where eminent talent is united to spotless virtue we are awed and dazzled into admiration, but our admiration is apt to be cold and reverential; while there is something in the harmless infirmities of a good and great but erring individual that pleads touchingly to our nature; and we turn more kindly towards the object of our idolatry when we find that, like ourselves, he is mortal and is frail. The epithet so often heard, and in such kindly tones, of " poor Goldsmith," speaks volumes. Few who consider the real compound of admirable and whimsical qualities which form his character would wish to prune away its eccentricities, trim its grotesque luxuriance, and clip it down to the decent formalities of rigid virtue. " Let not his frailties be remembered," said Johnson; " he was a very great man." But, for our part, we rather say " Let them be remembered," since their tendency is to endear; and we question whether he himself would not feel gratified in hearing his reader, after dwelling with admiration on the proofs of his greatness, close the volume with the kind-hearted phrase, so fondly and familiarly ejaculated, of " POOR GOLDSMITH!"

I am Dear Sir with the greatest esteem your most obedient humble servant;

Oliver Goldsmith.

THE TRAVELLER.

REV. HENRY GOLDSMITH.

Dear Sir,

I am sensible that the friendship between us can acquire no new force from the ceremonies of a dedication; and perhaps it demands an excuse thus to prefix your name to my attempts, which you decline giving with your own. But as a part of this poem was formerly written to you from Switzerland, the whole can now, with propriety, be only inscribed to you. It will also throw a light upon many parts of it, when the reader understands that it is addressed to a man who, despising fame and fortune, has retired early to happiness and obscurity with an income of forty pounds a year.

I now perceive, my dear brother, the wisdom of your humble choice. You have entered upon a sacred office, where the harvest is great and the labourers are but few; while you have left the field of ambition, where the labourers are many and the harvest not worth carrying away. But of all kinds of ambition—what from the refinement of the times, from differing systems of criticism, and from the divisions of party —that which pursues poetical fame is the wildest.

Poetry makes a principal amusement among unpolished nations; but in a country verging to the extremes of refinement, painting and music come in for a share. As these offer the feeble mind a less laborious entertainment, they at first rival poetry, and at length supplant her: they engross all that favour once shown to her; and, though but younger sisters, seize upon the elder's birthright.

Yet, however this art may be neglected by the powerful, it is still in greater danger from the mistaken efforts of the

D

learned to improve it. What criticisms have we not heard of late in favour of blank verse and pindaric odes, choruses, anapests and iambics, alliterative care and happy negligence! Every absurdity has now a champion to defend it; and as he is generally much in the wrong, so he has always much to say—for error is ever talkative.

But there is an enemy to this art still more dangerous: I mean party. Party entirely distorts the judgment and destroys the taste. When the mind is once infected with this disease, it can only find pleasure in what contributes to increase the distemper. Like the tiger, that seldom desists from pursuing man after having once preyed upon human flesh, the reader who has once gratified his appetite with calumny makes ever after the most agreeable feast upon murdered reputation. Such readers generally admire some half-witted thing, who wants to be thought a bold man, having lost the character of a wise one. Him they dignify with the name of poet: his tawdry lampoons are called satires; his turbulence is said to be force, and his frenzy fire.

What reception a poem may find which has neither abuse, party, nor blank verse to support it, I cannot tell; nor am I solicitous to know. My aims are right. Without espousing the cause of any party, I have attempted to moderate the rage of all. I have endeavoured to show that there may be equal happiness in states that are differently governed from our own; that every state has a particular principle of happiness; and that this principle in each may be carried to a mischievous excess. There are few can judge better than yourself how far these positions are illustrated in this poem.

　　　I am, Dear Sir,
　　　　　　Your most affectionate brother,
　　　　　　　　　　OLIVER GOLDSMITH.

THE TRAVELLER;

OR,

A PROSPECT OF SOCIETY.

REMOTE, unfriended, melancholy, slow—
Or by the lazy Scheldt or wandering Po,
Or onward where the rude Carinthian boor
Against the houseless stranger shuts the door,
Or where Campania's plain forsaken lies
A weary waste expanding to the skies—

Where'er I roam, whatever realms to see,
My heart, untravell'd, fondly turns to thee;
Still to my Brother turns, with ceaseless pain,
And drags at each remove a lengthening chain.   10
  Eternal blessings crown my earliest friend,
And round his dwelling guardian saints attend:
Blest be that spot, where cheerful guests retire
To pause from toil, and trim their evening fire;
Blest that abode, where want and pain repair,
And every stranger finds a ready chair;
Blest be those feasts with simple plenty crown'd,
Where all the ruddy family around
Laugh at the jests or pranks that never fail,
Or sigh with pity at some mournful tale,   20
Or press the bashful stranger to his food,
And learn the luxury of doing good.
  But me, not destin'd such delights to share,
My prime of life in wandering spent and care—
Impell'd with steps unceasing to pursue
Some fleeting good that mocks me with the view,
That, like the circle bounding earth and skies,
Allures from far, yet, as I follow, flies—
My fortune leads to traverse realms alone,
And find no spot of all the world my own.   30
  Even now, where Alpine solitudes ascend,
I sit me down a pensive hour to spend;
And placed on high, above the storm's career,
Look downward where an hundred realms appear—
Lakes, forests, cities, plains extending wide,
The pomp of kings, the shepherd's humbler pride.
  When thus Creation's charms around combine,
Amidst the store should thankless pride repine?
Say, should the philosophic mind disdain
That good which makes each humbler bosom vain?   40
Let school-taught pride dissemble all it can,

These little things are great to little man;
And wiser he whose sympathetic mind
Exults in all the good of all mankind.
Ye glittering towns, with wealth and splendour crown'd,
Ye fields, where summer spreads profusion round,
Ye lakes, whose vessels catch the busy gale,
Ye bending swains, that dress the flowery vale—
For me your tributary stores combine;
Creation's heir, the world, the world is mine!   50

As some lone miser, visiting his store,
Bends at his treasure, counts, recounts it o'er—
Hoards after hoards his rising raptures fill,
Yet still he sighs, for hoards are wanting still—
Thus to my breast alternate passions rise,
Pleas'd with each good that Heaven to man supplies,

Yet oft a sigh prevails, and sorrows fall,
To see the hoard of human bliss so small;
And oft I wish, amidst the scene, to find
Some spot to real happiness consign'd,　　　　60
Where my worn soul, each wandering hope at rest,
May gather bliss to see my fellows blest.
　But where to find that happiest spot below,
Who can direct, when all pretend to know?
The shuddering tenant of the frigid zone
Boldly proclaims that happiest spot his own,
Extols the treasures of his stormy seas,
And his long nights of revelry and ease;
The naked negro, panting at the line,
Boasts of his golden sands and palmy wine,　　70
Basks in the glare, or stems the tepid wave,
And thanks his gods for all the good they gave.
Such is the patriot's boast, where'er we roam;
His first, best country ever is at home.
And yet, perhaps, if countries we compare,
And estimate the blessings which they share,
Though patriots flatter, still shall wisdom find
An equal portion dealt to all mankind;
As different good, by art or nature given,
To different nations makes their blessings even.　　80
　Nature, a mother kind alike to all,
Still grants her bliss at Labour's earnest call:
With food as well the peasant is supplied
On Idra's cliffs as Arno's shelvy side;
And though the rocky crested summits frown,
These rocks, by custom, turn to beds of down.
From Art more various are the blessings sent—
Wealth, commerce, honour, liberty, content;
Yet these each other's power so strong contest
That either seems destructive of the rest:
Where wealth and freedom reign contentment fails,

And honour sinks where commerce long prevails.
Hence every state, to one lov'd blessing prone,
Conforms and models life to that alone :
Each to the favourite happiness attends,
And spurns the plan that aims at other ends;
Till, carried to excess in each domain,
This favourite good begets peculiar pain.

But let us try these truths with closer eyes,
And trace them through the prospect as it lies :   100
Here for a while my proper cares resign'd,
Here let me sit in sorrow for mankind;
Like yon neglected shrub, at random cast,
That shades the steep, and sighs at every blast.

Far to the right, where Apennine ascends,
Bright as the summer, Italy extends;
Its uplands sloping deck the mountain's side,
Woods over woods in gay theatric pride,
While oft some temple's mouldering tops between
With venerable grandeur mark the scene.   110

Could Nature's bounty satisfy the breast,
The sons of Italy were surely blest.
Whatever fruits in different climes were found,
That proudly rise, or humbly court the ground;
Whatever blooms in torrid tracts appear,
Whose bright succession decks the varied year;
Whatever sweets salute the northern sky
With vernal lives, that blossom but to die;
These, here disporting, own the kindred soil,
Nor ask luxuriance from the planter's toil;   120
While sea-born gales their gelid wings expand
To winnow fragrance round the smiling land.

But small the bliss that sense alone bestows,
And sensual bliss is all the nation knows;
In florid beauty groves and fields appear—
Man seems the only growth that dwindles here.

Contrasted faults through all his manners reign:
Though poor, luxurious; though submissive, vain;
Though grave, yet trifling; zealous, yet untrue;
And even in penance planning sins anew.   130
All evils here contaminate the mind,
That opulence departed leaves behind;

For wealth was theirs—not far remov'd the date
When commerce proudly flourish'd through the state.
At her command the palace learn'd to rise,
Again the long-fallen column sought the skies,
The canvas glow'd beyond even nature warm,
The pregnant quarry teem'd with human form,
Till, more unsteady than the southern gale,
Commerce on other shores display'd her sail; 140
While nought remain'd of all that riches gave,
But towns unmann'd and lords without a slave:
And late the nation found, with fruitless skill,
Its former strength was but plethoric ill.

 Yet still the loss of wealth is here supplied
By arts, the splendid wrecks of former pride:
From these the feeble heart and long-fallen mind

An easy compensation seem to find.
Here may be seen, in bloodless pomp array'd,
The pasteboard triumph and the cavalcade,   150
Processions form'd for piety and love,
A mistress or a saint in every grove.
By sports like these are all their cares beguil'd;
The sports of children satisfy the child.
Each nobler aim, represt by long control,
Now sinks at last, or feebly mans the soul;
While low delights, succeeding fast behind,
In happier meanness occupy the mind:
As in those domes, where Cæsars once bore sway,
Defac'd by time and tottering in decay,   160
There in the ruin, heedless of the dead,
The shelter-seeking peasant builds his shed;
And, wondering man could want the larger pile,
Exults, and owns his cottage with a smile.

My soul, turn from them, turn we to survey
Where rougher climes a nobler race display,
Where the bleak Swiss their stormy mansions tread,
And force a churlish soil for scanty bread.
No product here the barren hills afford
But man and steel, the soldier and his sword;   170
No vernal blooms their torpid rocks array,
But winter lingering chills the lap of May;
No zephyr fondly sues the mountain's breast,
But meteors glare, and stormy glooms invest

Yet still, even here, content can spread a charm,
Redress the clime, and all its rage disarm.
Though poor the peasant's hut, his feasts though small,
He sees his little lot the lot of all;
Sees no contiguous palace rear its head,
To shame the meanness of his humble shed,   180
No costly lord the sumptuous banquet deal,
To make him loathe his vegetable meal;

But calm, and bred in ignorance and toil,
Each wish contracting, fits him to the soil.
Cheerful at morn, he wakes from short repose,
Breasts the keen air, and carols as he goes;
With patient angle trolls the finny deep,
Or drives his venturous ploughshare to the steep;
Or seeks the den where snow-tracks mark the way,
And drags the struggling savage into day.
At night returning, every labour sped,
He sits him down the monarch of a shed;
Smiles by his cheerful fire, and round surveys
His children's looks, that brighten at the blaze;
While his lov'd partner, boastful of her hoard,
Displays her cleanly platter on the board:
And haply too some pilgrim, thither led,
With many a tale repays the nightly bed.

190

Thus every good his native wilds impart
Imprints the patriot passion on his heart;   200
And even those ills that round his mansion rise
Enhance the bliss his scanty fund supplies.
Dear is that shed to which his soul conforms,
And dear that hill which lifts him to the storms;
And as a child, when scaring sounds molest,
Clings close and closer to the mother's breast,
So the loud torrent and the whirlwind's roar
But bind him to his native mountains more.
  Such are the charms to barren states assign'd;
Their wants but few, their wishes all confin'd.   210
Yet let them only share the praises due;
If few their wants, their pleasures are but few:
For every want that stimulates the breast
Becomes a source of pleasure when redrest.
Whence from such lands each pleasing science flies,
That first excites desire, and then supplies.
Unknown to them, when sensual pleasures cloy,
To fill the languid pause with finer joy;
Unknown those powers that raise the soul to flame,

Catch every nerve, and vibrate through the frame :   220
Their level life is but a smouldering fire,
Unquench'd by want, unfann'd by strong desire ;
Unfit for raptures, or, if raptures cheer
On some high festival of once a year,
In wild excess the vulgar breast takes fire,
Till, buried in debauch, the bliss expire.
  But not their joys alone thus coarsely flow ;
Their morals, like their pleasures, are but low :
For, as refinement stops, from sire to son
Unalter'd, unimprov'd the manners run ;   230

And love's and friendship's finely pointed dart
Fall blunted from each indurated heart.
Some sterner virtues o'er the mountain's breast
May sit, like falcons cowering on the nest;
But all the gentler morals, such as play
Through life's more cultur'd walks, and charm the way.
These, far dispers'd, on timorous pinions fly,
To sport and flutter in a kinder sky.

To kinder skies, where gentler manners reign,
I turn; and France displays her bright domain.   240
Gay, sprightly land of mirth and social ease,
Pleas'd with thyself, whom all the world can please,
How often have I led thy sportive choir,
With tuneless pipe, beside the murmuring Loire,
Where shading elms along the margin grew,
And, freshen'd from the wave, the zephyr flew!
And haply, though my harsh touch, faltering still,
But mock'd all tune, and marr'd the dancer's skill,
Yet would the village praise my wondrous power,
And dance, forgetful of the noontide hour.   250
Alike all ages: dames of ancient days
Have led their children through the mirthful maze;
And the gay grandsire, skill'd in gestic lore,
Has frisk'd beneath the burthen of threescore.

So blest a life these thoughtless realms display;
Thus idly busy rolls their world away.
Theirs are those arts that mind to mind endear,
For honour forms the social temper here:
Honour, that praise which real merit gains,
Or even imaginary worth obtains,   260
Here passes current; paid from hand to hand,
It shifts, in splendid traffic, round the land;
From courts to camps, to cottages it strays,
And all are taught an avarice of praise.
They please, are pleas'd; they give to get esteem,
Till, seeming blest, they grow to what they seem.

But while this softer art their bliss supplies,
It gives their follies also room to rise;
For praise, too dearly lov'd, or warmly sought,
Enfeebles all internal strength of thought;   270
And the weak soul, within itself unblest,
Leans for all pleasure on another's breast.
Hence ostentation here, with tawdry art,
Pants for the vulgar praise which fools impart;
Here vanity assumes her pert grimace,
And trims her robes of frieze with copper lace;
Here beggar pride defrauds her daily cheer,
To boast one splendid banquet once a year:
The mind still turns where shifting fashion draws,
Nor weighs the solid worth of self-applause.   280
   To men of other minds my fancy flies,
Embosom'd in the deep where Holland lies.
Methinks her patient sons before me stand,
Where the broad ocean leans against the land,
And, sedulous to stop the coming tide,
Lift the tall rampire's artificial pride.
Onward, methinks, and diligently slow,
The firm, connected bulwark seems to grow,
Spreads its long arms amid the watery roar,
Scoops out an empire, and usurps the shore;   290
While the pent ocean, rising o'er the pile,
Sees an amphibious world beneath him smile—
The slow canal, the yellow-blossom'd vale,
The willow-tufted bank, the gliding sail,
The crowded mart, the cultivated plain—
A new creation rescued from his reign.
   Thus, while around the wave-subjected soil
Impels the native to repeated toil,
Industrious habits in each bosom reign,
And industry begets a love of gain.   300
Hence all the good from opulence that springs,

With all those ills superfluous treasure brings,
Are here display'd. Their much-lov'd wealth imparts
Convenience, plenty, elegance, and arts;
But view them closer, craft and fraud appear,
Even liberty itself is barter'd here.
At gold's superior charms all freedom flies;
The needy sell it, and the rich man buys:
A land of tyrants, and a den of slaves,
Here wretches seek dishonourable graves,   310
And, calmly bent, to servitude conform,
Dull as their lakes that slumber in the storm.
    Heavens! how unlike their Belgic sires of old—
Rough, poor, content, ungovernably bold,
War in each breast, and freedom on each brow!
How much unlike the sons of Britain now!

Fir'd at the sound, my genius spreads her wing,
And flies where Britain courts the western spring;
Where lawns extend that scorn Arcadian pride,
And brighter streams than fam'd Hydaspes glide.   320
There, all around, the gentlest breezes stray;
There gentle music melts on every spray;
Creation's mildest charms are there combin'd:
Extremes are only in the master's mind.
Stern o'er each bosom reason holds her state,
With daring aims irregularly great.
Pride in their port, defiance in their eye,
I see the lords of human kind pass by;
Intent on high designs, a thoughtful band,
By forms unfashion'd, fresh from Nature's hand,   330
Fierce in their native hardiness of soul,
True to imagin'd right, above control;

E

While even the peasant boasts these rights to scan,
And learns to venerate himself as man.
　　Thine, Freedom, thine the blessings pictur'd here,
Thine are those charms that dazzle and endear;
Too blest indeed were such without alloy,
But, foster'd even by freedom, ills annoy.
That independence Britons prize too high
Keeps man from man, and breaks the social tie:　　340
The self-dependent lordlings stand alone,
All claims that bind and sweeten life unknown.
Here, by the bonds of nature feebly held,
Minds combat minds, repelling and repell'd;
Ferments arise, imprison'd factions roar,
Represt ambition struggles round her shore,
Till, overwrought, the general system feels
Its motions stop, or frenzy fire the wheels.
　　Nor this the worst.　As Nature's ties decay,
As duty, love, and honour fail to sway,　　350
Fictitious bonds, the bonds of wealth and law,
Still gather strength, and force unwilling awe.
Hence all obedience bows to these alone,
And talent sinks, and merit weeps unknown;
Till time may come when, stript of all her charms,
The land of scholars, and the nurse of arms,
Where noble stems transmit the patriot flame,
Where kings have toil'd, and poets wrote for fame,
One sink of level avarice shall lie,
And scholars, soldiers, kings, unhonour'd die.　　360
　　Yet think not, thus when Freedom's ills I state,
I mean to flatter kings or court the great.
Ye powers of truth, that bid my soul aspire,
Far from my bosom drive the low desire!
And thou, fair Freedom, taught alike to feel
The rabble's rage and tyrant's angry steel;
Thou transitory flower, alike undone

By proud contempt or favour's fostering sun,
Still may thy blooms the changeful clime endure!
I only would repress them to secure: 370
For just experience tells, in every soil,
That those who think must govern those that toil;
And all that Freedom's highest aims can reach
Is but to lay proportion'd loads on each.
Hence, should one order disproportion'd grow,
Its double weight must ruin all below.
    O then how blind to all that truth requires,
Who think it freedom when a part aspires!
Calm is my soul, nor apt to rise in arms,
Except when fast-approaching danger warms: 380
But, when contending chiefs blockade the throne,

Contracting regal power to stretch their own;
When I behold a factious band agree
To call it freedom when themselves are free;
Each wanton judge new penal statutes draw,
Laws grind the poor, and rich men rule the law;
The wealth of climes where savage nations roam
Pillag'd from slaves to purchase slaves at home;
Fear, pity, justice, indignation start,
Tear off reserve, and bare my swelling heart: 390
Till half a patriot, half a coward grown,
I fly from petty tyrants to the throne.
 Yes, Brother, curse with me that baleful hour
When first ambition struck at regal power;
And thus, polluting honour in its source,
Gave wealth to sway the mind with double force.
Have we not seen, round Britain's peopled shore,
Her useful sons exchang'd for useless ore?
Seen all her triumphs but destruction haste,
Like flaring tapers brightening as they waste?   400
Seen opulence, her grandeur to maintain,
Lead stern depopulation in her train,
And over fields where scatter'd hamlets rose,
In barren, solitary pomp repose?
Have we not seen, at pleasure's lordly call,
The smiling, long-frequented village fall?
Beheld the duteous son, the sire decay'd,
The modest matron, and the blushing maid,
Forc'd from their homes, a melancholy train,
To traverse climes beyond the western main;   410
Where wild Oswego spreads her swamps around,
And Niagara stuns with thundering sound?
 Even now, perhaps, as there some pilgrim strays
Through tangled forests, and through dangerous ways,
Where beasts with man divided empire claim,
And the brown Indian marks with murderous aim;

There, while above the giddy tempest flies,
And all around distressful yells arise,
The pensive exile, bending with his woe,
To stop too fearful, and too faint to go,   420
Casts a long look where England's glories shine,
And bids his bosom sympathize with mine.
  Vain, very vain, my weary search to find
That bliss which only centres in the mind:

Why have I stray'd from pleasure and repose,
To seek a good each government bestows?
In every government, though terrors reign,
Though tyrant kings or tyrant laws restrain,
How small, of all that human hearts endure,
That part which laws or kings can cause or cure !   43c
Still to ourselves in every place consign'd,
Our own felicity we make or find :
With secret course, which no loud storms annoy,
Glides the smooth current of domestic joy.
The lifted ax, the agonizing wheel,
Luke's iron crown, and Damiens' bed of steel,
To men remote from power but rarely known,
Leave reason, faith, and conscience, all our own.

THE DESERTED VILLAGE.

SIR JOSHUA REYNOLDS.

DEAR SIR,

I can have no expectations, in an address of this kind, either to add to your reputation or to establish my own. You can gain nothing from my admiration, as I am ignorant of that art in which you are said to excel; and I may lose much by the severity of your judgment, as few have a juster taste in poetry than you. Setting interest therefore aside, to which I never paid much attention, I must be indulged at present in following my affections. The only dedication I ever made was to my brother, because I loved him better than most other men. He is since dead. Permit me to inscribe this poem to you.

How far you may be pleased with the versification and mere mechanical parts of this attempt I do not pretend to inquire; but I know you will object—and indeed several of our best and wisest friends concur in the opinion—that the depopulation it deplores is nowhere to be seen, and the disorders it laments are only to be found in the poet's own imagination. To this I can scarce make any other answer than that I sincerely believe what I have written; that I have taken all possible pains, in my country excursions for these four or five years past, to be certain of what I allege; and that all my views and inquiries have led me to believe those miseries real which I here attempt to display. But this is not the place to enter into an inquiry whether the country be depopulating or not; the discussion would take up much room, and I should prove myself, at best, an indifferent politician to tire the reader with a long preface when I want his unfatigued attention to a long poem.

In regretting the depopulation of the country, I inveigh against the increase of our luxuries; and here I also expect the shout of modern politicians against me. For twenty or thirty years past it has been the fashion to consider luxury as one of the greatest national advantages; and all the wisdom of antiquity, in that particular, as erroneous. Still, however, I must remain a professed ancient on that head, and continue to think those luxuries prejudicial to states by which so many vices are introduced and so many kingdoms have been undone. Indeed, so much has been poured out of late on the other side of the question, that merely for the sake of novelty and variety one would sometimes wish to be in the right.

   I am, Dear Sir,

     Your sincere friend,

      and ardent admirer,

       OLIVER GOLDSMITH.

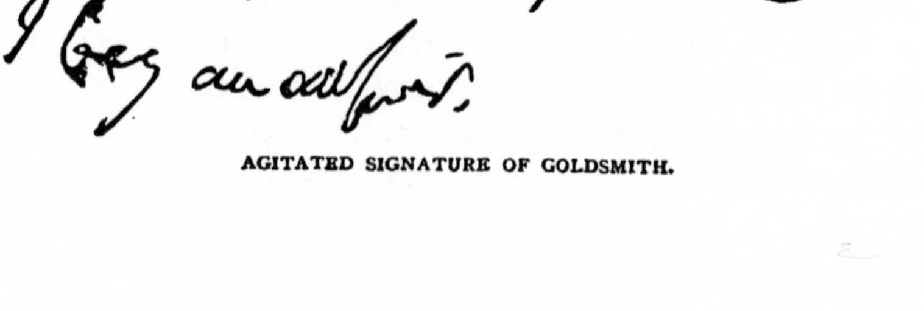

AGITATED SIGNATURE OF GOLDSMITH.

THE DESERTED VILLAGE

SWEET AUBURN! loveliest village of the plain,
Where health and plenty cheer'd the labouring swain,
Where smiling spring its earliest visit paid,
And parting summer's lingering blooms delay'd;
Dear lovely bowers of innocence and ease,
Seats of my youth, when every sport could please,
How often have I loiter'd o'er thy green,
Where humble happiness endear'd each scene
How often have I paus'd on every charm,
The shelter'd cot, the cultivated farm,

10

The never-failing brook, the busy mill,
The decent church that topt the neighbouring hill,
The hawthorn bush with seats beneath the shade,
For talking age and whispering lovers made!
How often have I blest the coming day
When toil remitting lent its turn to play,
And all the village train from labour free,
Led up their sports beneath the spreading tree;
While many a pastime circled in the shade,
The young contending as the old survey'd,   20
And many a gambol frolick'd o'er the ground,
And sleights of art and feats of strength went round!
And still, as each repeated pleasure tir'd,
Succeeding sports the mirthful band inspir'd;
The dancing pair that simply sought renown
By holding out to tire each other down,
The swain mistrustless of his smutted face
While secret laughter titter'd round the place,
The bashful virgin's sidelong looks of love,
The matron's glance that would those looks reprove.   30
These were thy charms, sweet village! sports like these,
With sweet succession, taught even toil to please;
These round thy bowers their cheerful influence shed;
These were thy charms—but all these charms are fled.
   Sweet smiling village, loveliest of the lawn,
Thy sports are fled, and all thy charms withdrawn;
Amidst thy bowers the tyrant's hand is seen,
And desolation saddens all thy green:
One only master grasps the whole domain,
And half a tillage stints thy smiling plain.   40
No more thy glassy brook reflects the day,
But chok'd with sedges works its weedy way;
Along thy glades, a solitary guest,
The hollow-sounding bittern guards its nest;
Amidst thy desert walks the lapwing flies,

And tires their echoes with unvaried cries;
Sunk are thy bowers in shapeless ruin all,
And the long grass o'ertops the mouldering wall;
And, trembling, shrinking from the spoiler's hand,
Far, far away thy children leave the land.   50

Ill fares the land, to hastening ills a prey,
Where wealth accumulates and men decay;
Princes and lords may flourish, or may fade—
A breath can make them, as a breath has made—
But a bold peasantry, their country's pride,
When once destroy'd, can never be supplied.

A time there was, ere England's griefs began,
When every rood of ground maintain'd its man:
For him light labour spread her wholesome store,
Just gave what life requir'd, but gave no more;   60
His best companions, innocence and health,
And his best riches, ignorance of wealth.

But times are alter'd; trade's unfeeling train
Usurp the land, and dispossess the swain:
Along the lawn where scatter'd hamlets rose,
Unwieldy wealth and cumbrous pomp repose,
And every want to opulence allied,
And every pang that folly pays to pride.
Those gentle hours that plenty bade to bloom,
Those calm desires that ask'd but little room,   70
Those healthful sports that grac'd the peaceful scene,
Liv'd in each look and brighten'd all the green—
These, far departing, seek a kinder shore,
And rural mirth and manners are no more.

Sweet Auburn! parent of the blissful hour,
Thy glades forlorn confess the tyrant's power.
Here, as I take my solitary rounds
Amidst thy tangling walks and ruin'd grounds,
And, many a year elaps'd, return to view
Where once the cottage stood, the hawthorn grew,   80

Remembrance wakes with all her busy train,
Swells at my breast, and turns the past to pain.
 In all my wanderings round this world of care,
In all my griefs—and God has given my share—
I still had hopes, my latest hours to crown,
Amidst these humble bowers to lay me down ;
To husband out life's taper at the close,
And keep the flame from wasting by repose.
I still had hopes, for pride attends us still,
Amidst the swains to show my book-learn'd skill,　　　90
Around my fire an evening group to draw,
And tell of all I felt, and all I saw;
And as an hare whom hounds and horns pursue
Pants to the place from whence at first she flew,
I still had hopes, my long vexations past,
Here to return—and die at home at last.
 O blest retirement, friend to life's decline,
Retreats from care, that never must be mine !
How happy he who crowns, in shades like these,
A youth of labour with an age of ease ;　　　100
Who quits a world where strong temptations try,
And, since 'tis hard to combat, learns to fly !
For him no wretches, born to work and weep,
Explore the mine, or tempt the dangerous deep ;
No surly porter stands, in guilty state,
To spurn imploring famine from the gate ;
But on he moves, to meet his latter end,
Angels around befriending virtue's friend,
Bends to the grave with unperceiv'd decay,
While resignation gently slopes the way,　　　110
And, all his prospects brightening to the last,
His heaven commences ere the world be past.
 Sweet was the sound, when oft at evening's close
Up yonder hill the village murmur rose.
There as I pass'd, with careless steps and slow,

The mingling notes came soften'd from below:
The swain responsive as the milkmaid sung,
The sober herd that low'd to meet their young,
The noisy geese that gabbled o'er the pool,
The playful children just let loose from school,   120
The watch-dog's voice that bay'd the whispering wind,
And the loud laugh that spoke the vacant mind—
These all in sweet confusion sought the shade,
And fill'd each pause the nightingale had made.
But now the sounds of population fail,
No cheerful murmurs fluctuate in the gale,
No busy steps the grass-grown footway tread,
For all the bloomy flush of life is fled—

All but yon widow'd, solitary thing,
That feebly bends beside the plashy spring ;   13c
She, wretched matron—forc'd in age, for bread,
To strip the brook with mantling cresses spread,
To pick her wintry faggot from the thorn,
To seek her nightly shed, and weep till morn—
She only left of all the harmless train,
The sad historian of the pensive plain !

Near yonder copse, where once the garden smil'd,
And still where many a garden-flower grows wild,
There, where a few torn shrubs the place disclose,
The village preacher's modest mansion rose.   14c
A man he was to all the country dear,
And passing rich with forty pounds a year.
Remote from towns he ran his godly race,
Nor e'er had chang'd, nor wish'd to change, his place ;
Unpractis'd he to fawn, or seek for power
By doctrines fashion'd to the varying hour ;
Far other aims his heart had learn'd to prize,

More skill'd to raise the wretched than to rise.
His house was known to all the vagrant train,
He chid their wanderings, but reliev'd their pain; 150
The long-remember'd beggar was his guest,
Whose beard descending swept his aged breast;
The ruin'd spendthrift, now no longer proud,
Claim'd kindred there, and had his claims allow'd;
The broken soldier, kindly bade to stay,
Sat by his fire, and talk'd the night away,
Wept o'er his wounds, or, tales of sorrow done,
Shoulder'd his crutch and show'd how fields were won.
Pleas'd with his guests, the good man learn'd to glow,
And quite forgot their vices in their woe; 160
Careless their merits or their faults to scan,
His pity gave ere charity began.
　　Thus to relieve the wretched was his pride,
And even his failings lean'd to virtue's side;
But in his duty prompt at every call,
He watch'd and wept, he pray'd and felt for all:
And, as a bird each fond endearment tries
To tempt its new-fledg'd offspring to the skies,
He tried each art, reprov'd each dull delay,
Allur'd to brighter worlds, and led the way. 170
　　Beside the bed where parting life was laid,
And sorrow, guilt, and pain by turns dismay'd,
The reverend champion stood : at his control
Despair and anguish fled the struggling soul;
Comfort came down the trembling wretch to raise,
And his last faltering accents whisper'd praise.
　　At church, with meek and unaffected grace,
His looks adorn'd the venerable place;
Truth from his lips prevail'd with double sway,
And fools who came to scoff remain'd to pray. 180
The service past, around the pious man,
With steady zeal, each honest rustic ran:

F

Even children follow'd, with endearing wile,
And pluck'd his gown, to share the good man's smile:
His ready smile a parent's warmth exprest,
Their welfare pleas'd him, and their cares distrest.
To them his heart, his love, his griefs were given,
But all his serious thoughts had rest in heaven:
As some tall cliff, that lifts its awful form,
Swells from the vale, and midway leaves the storm,   190

Though round its breast the rolling clouds are spread,
Eternal sunshine settles on its head.
　Beside yon straggling fence that skirts the way,
With blossom'd furze unprofitably gay,
There, in his noisy mansion, skill'd to rule,
The village master taught his little school.

A man severe he was, and stern to view;
I knew him well, and every truant knew:
Well had the boding tremblers learn'd to trace
The day's disasters in his morning face;　　　200
Full well they laugh'd with counterfeited glee
At all his jokes, for many a joke had he;
Full well the busy whisper, circling round,
Convey'd the dismal tidings when he frown'd.
Yet he was kind, or if severe in aught,
The love he bore to learning was in fault.
The village all declar'd how much he knew;
'Twas certain he could write, and cipher too,
Lands he could measure, terms and tides presage,
And even the story ran that he could gauge.　　210
In arguing too, the parson own'd his skill,
For even though vanquish'd he could argue still;
While words of learned length and thundering sound
Amaz'd the gazing rustics rang'd around;
And still they gaz'd, and still the wonder grew
That one small head could carry all he knew.
　　But past is all his fame: the very spot,
Where many a time he triumph'd, is forgot.
Near yonder thorn, that lifts its head on high,
Where once the sign-post caught the passing eye,　220
Low lies that house where nut-brown draughts inspir'd,
Where gray-beard mirth and smiling toil retir'd,
Where village statesmen talk'd with looks profound,
And news much older than their ale went round.
Imagination fondly stoops to trace
The parlour splendours of that festive place:
The whitewash'd wall, the nicely sanded floor,
The varnish'd clock that click'd behind the door;
The chest contriv'd a double debt to pay,
A bed by night, a chest of drawers by day;　　230
The pictures plac'd for ornament and use.

The twelve good rules, the royal game of goose;
The hearth, except when winter chill'd the day,
With aspen boughs, and flowers, and fennel gay,
While broken tea-cups, wisely kept for show,
Rang'd o'er the chimney, glisten'd in a row.
    Vain, transitory splendours! could not all
Reprieve the tottering mansion from its fall?
Obscure it sinks, nor shall it more impart
An hour's importance to the poor man's heart.   240

Thither no more the peasant shall repair
To sweet oblivion of his daily care;
No more the farmer's news, the barber's tale,
No more the woodman's ballad shall prevail;
No more the smith his dusky brow shall clear,
Relax his ponderous strength, and lean to hear;
The host himself no longer shall be found
Careful to see the mantling bliss go round;
Nor the coy maid, half willing to be prest,
Shall kiss the cup to pass it to the rest.   25c
    Yes! let the rich deride, the proud disdain,
These simple blessings of the lowly train;
To me more dear, congenial to my heart,

One native charm, than all the gloss of art.
Spontaneous joys, where nature has its play,
The soul adopts, and owns their first-born sway;
Lightly they frolic o'er the vacant mind,
Unenvied, unmolested, unconfin'd.
But the long pomp, the midnight masquerade,
With all the freaks of wanton wealth array'd,   260
In these, ere triflers half their wish obtain,
The toiling pleasure sickens into pain;
And, even while fashion's brightest arts decoy,
The heart distrusting asks, if this be joy.

Ye friends to truth, ye statesmen who survey
The rich man's joys increase, the poor's decay,
'Tis yours to judge how wide the limits stand
Between a splendid and an happy land.
Proud swells the tide with loads of freighted ore,
And shouting Folly hails them from her shore;   270
Hoards even beyond the miser's wish abound,
And rich men flock from all the world around;
Yet count our gains: this wealth is but a name
That leaves our useful products still the same.
Not so the loss.   The man of wealth and pride
Takes up a space that many poor supplied—
Space for his lake, his park's extended bounds,
Space for his horses, equipage, and hounds:
The robe that wraps his limbs in silken sloth
Has robb'd the neighbouring fields of half their growth; 280
His seat, where solitary sports are seen,
Indignant spurns the cottage from the green;
Around the world each needful product flies,
For all the luxuries the world supplies.
While thus the land adorn'd for pleasure, all
In barren splendour feebly waits the fall.

As some fair female, unadorn'd and plain,
Secure to please while youth confirms her reign,

Slights every borrow'd charm that dress supplies,
Nor shares with art the triumph of her eyes;   290
But when those charms are past, for charms are frail,
When time advances, and when lovers fail,
She then shines forth, solicitous to bless,
In all the glaring impotence of dress:
Thus fares the land, by luxury betray'd;
In nature's simplest charms at first array'd,
But verging to decline, its splendours rise,
Its vistas strike, its palaces surprise;
While, scourg'd by famine from the smiling land,
The mournful peasant leads his humble band;   300
And while he sinks, without one arm to save,
The country blooms—a garden, and a grave.

Where then, ah! where shall poverty reside,
To scape the pressure of contiguous pride?
If to some common's fenceless limits stray'd
He drives his flock to pick the scanty blade,
Those fenceless fields the sons of wealth divide,
And even the bare-worn common is denied.
    If to the city sped—what waits him there?
To see profusion that he must not share;   310
To see ten thousand baneful arts combin'd

To pamper luxury, and thin mankind;
To see those joys the sons of pleasure know,
Extorted from his fellow-creatures' woe.
Here, while the courtier glitters in brocade,
There the pale artist plies the sickly trade;
Here, while the proud their long-drawn pomps display,
There the black gibbet glooms beside the way.
The dome where pleasure holds her midnight reign,
Here, richly deck'd, admits the gorgeous train;   320
Tumultuous grandeur crowds the blazing square,
The rattling chariots clash, the torches glare.
Sure scenes like these no troubles e'er annoy!
Sure these denote one universal joy!
Are these thy serious thoughts?   Ah, turn thine eyes
Where the poor houseless shivering female lies.

She once, perhaps, in village plenty blest,
Has wept at tales of innocence distrest;
Her modest looks the cottage might adorn,
Sweet as the primrose peeps beneath the thorn;   330
Now lost to all—her friends, her virtue fled—
Near her betrayer's door she lays her head,
And, pinch'd with cold, and shrinking from the shower,
With heavy heart deplores that luckless hour
When idly first, ambitious of the town,
She left her wheel, and robes of country brown.
　　Do thine, sweet Auburn, thine, the loveliest train,
Do thy fair tribes participate her pain?
Even now, perhaps, by cold and hunger led,
At proud men's doors they ask a little bread.   340
Ah, no! To distant climes, a dreary scene,
Where half the convex world intrudes between,
Through torrid tracts with fainting steps they go,
Where wild Altama murmurs to their woe.
Far different there from all that charm'd before,
The various terrors of that horrid shore:
Those blazing suns that dart a downward ray,
And fiercely shed intolerable day;
Those matted woods where birds forget to sing,
But silent bats in drowsy clusters cling;   350
Those poisonous fields with rank luxuriance crown'd,
Where the dark scorpion gathers death around;
Where at each step the stranger fears to wake
The rattling terrors of the vengeful snake;
Where crouching tigers wait their hapless prey,
And savage men more murderous still than they;
While oft in whirls the mad tornado flies,
Mingling the ravag'd landscape with the skies.
Far different these from every former scene;
The cooling brook, the grassy-vested green,   360
The breezy covert of the warbling grove,
That only shelter'd thefts of harmless love.

Good Heaven! what sorrows gloom'd that parting day,
That call'd them from their native walks away;
When the poor exiles, every pleasure past,
Hung round the bowers, and fondly look'd their last,
And took a long farewell, and wish'd in vain
For seats like these beyond the western main;
And shuddering still to face the distant deep,
Return'd and wept, and still return'd to weep.   370
The good old sire the first prepar'd to go
To new-found worlds, and wept for others' woe;
But for himself, in conscious virtue brave,
He only wish'd for worlds beyond the grave.
His lovely daughter, lovelier in her tears,
The fond companion of his helpless years,

Silent went next, neglectful of her charms,
And left a lover's for a father's arms.
With louder plaints the mother spoke her woes,
And blest the cot where every pleasure rose,   380
And kiss'd her thoughtless babes with many a tear,
And clasp'd them close, in sorrow doubly dear;
While her fond husband strove to lend relief
In all the silent manliness of grief.
    O Luxury! thou curst by Heaven's decree,

How ill exchang'd are things like these for thee !
How do thy potions, with insidious joy,
Diffuse their pleasures only to destroy!
Kingdoms by thee, to sickly greatness grown,
Boast of a florid vigour not their own :   390
At every draught more large and large they grow,
A bloated mass of rank, unwieldy woe;
Till sapp'd their strength, and every part unsound,
Down, down they sink, and spread a ruin round.
   Even now the devastation is begun,
And half the business of destruction done;
Even now, methinks, as pondering here I stand,
I see the rural Virtues leave the land.
Down where yon anchoring vessel spreads the sail,
That idly waiting flaps with every gale,   400
Downward they move, a melancholy band,
Pass from the shore, and darken all the strand.
Contented Toil and hospitable Care,
And kind connubial Tenderness, are there;
And Piety with wishes plac'd above,
And steady Loyalty, and faithful Love.
And thou, sweet Poetry, thou loveliest maid,
Still first to fly where sensual joys invade,
Unfit in these degenerate times of shame
To catch the heart, or strike for honest fame ;   410
Dear, charming nymph, neglected and decried,
My shame in crowds, my solitary pride,
Thou source of all my bliss, and all my woe,
That found'st me poor at first, and keep'st me so,
Thou guide by which the nobler arts excel,
Thou nurse of every virtue, fare thee well!
Farewell! and O where'er thy voice be tried,
On Torno's cliffs or Pambamarca's side,
Whether where equinoctial fervours glow,
Or winter wraps the polar world in snow,   420

Still let thy voice, prevailing over time,
Redress the rigours of the inclement clime;
Aid slighted truth with thy persuasive strain;
Teach erring man to spurn the rage of gain;
Teach him, that states of native strength possest,
Though very poor, may still be very blest;
That trade's proud empire hastes to swift decay,
As ocean sweeps the labour'd mole away;
While self-dependent power can time defy,
As rocks resist the billows and the sky.

43c

RETALIATION.

G

RETALIATION:

INCLUDING

EPITAPHS ON THE MOST DISTINGUISHED WITS OF THIS METROPOLIS.

OF old, when Scarron his companions invited,
Each guest brought his dish, and the feast was united;
If our landlord supplies us with beef and with fish,
Let each guest bring himself—and he brings the best dish:
Our dean shall be venison, just fresh from the plains;
Our Burke shall be tongue, with a garnish of brains;
Our Will shall be wild fowl, of excellent flavour,
And Dick with his pepper shall heighten their savour;
Our Cumberland's sweetbread its place shall obtain;
And Douglas is pudding, substantial and plain;   10
Our Garrick's a salad, for in him we see
Oil, vinegar, sugar, and saltness agree;
To make out the dinner, full certain I am,
That Ridge is anchovy, and Reynolds is lamb;
That Hickey's a capon; and, by the same rule,
Magnanimous Goldsmith a gooseberry fool.
At a dinner so various, at such a repast,
Who'd not be a glutton, and stick to the last?
Here, waiter, more wine! let me sit while I'm able,
Till all my companions sink under the table;   20
Then, with chaos and blunders encircling my head,
Let me ponder, and tell what I think of the dead.

Here lies the good dean, reunited to earth,
Who mix'd reason with pleasure, and wisdom with mirth:
If he had any faults, he has left us in doubt—
At least, in six weeks, I could not find 'em out;
Yet some have declar'd, and it can't be denied 'em,
That sly-boots was cursedly cunning to hide 'em.
　　Here lies our good Edmund, whose genius was such.
We scarcely can praise it, or blame it too much;　　　　30
Who, born for the universe, narrow'd his mind,
And to party gave up what was meant for mankind;
Though fraught with all learning, yet straining his throat
To persuade Tommy Townshend to lend him a vote;
Who, too deep for his hearers, still went on refining,
And thought of convincing, while they thought of dining;
Though equal to all things, for all things unfit;
Too nice for a statesman, too proud for a wit,
For a patriot too cool, for a drudge disobedient,
And too fond of the *right* to pursue the *expedient.*　　　40
In short 'twas his fate, unemploy'd, or in place, sir,
To eat mutton cold, and cut blocks with a razor.
　　Here lies honest William, whose heart was a mint,
While the owner ne'er knew half the good that was in't:
The pupil of impulse, it forc'd him along,
His conduct still right, with his argument wrong;
Still aiming at honour, yet fearing to roam—
The coachman was tipsy, the chariot drove home.
Would you ask for his merits? alas! he had none;
What was good was spontaneous, his faults were his own.　　50
　　Here lies honest Richard, whose fate I must sigh at;
Alas, that such frolic should now be so quiet!
What spirits were his! what wit and what whim!
Now breaking a jest, and now breaking a limb;
Now wrangling and grumbling to keep up the ball;
Now teasing and vexing, yet laughing at all!
In short, so provoking a devil was Dick,

That we wished him full ten times a-day at Old Nick;
But, missing his mirth and agreeable vein,
As often we wish'd to have Dick back again.   60
 Here Cumberland lies, having acted his parts,
The Terence of England, the mender of hearts;
A flattering painter, who made it his care
To draw men as they ought to be, not as they are.
His gallants are all faultless, his women divine,
And comedy wonders at being so fine;
Like a tragedy queen he has dizen'd her out,
Or rather like tragedy giving a rout.
His fools have their follies so lost in a crowd
Of virtues and feelings, that folly grows proud;   70
And coxcombs, alike in their failings alone,
Adopting his portraits, are pleas'd with their own.
Say, where has our poet this malady caught?
Or wherefore his characters thus without fault?
Say, was it that vainly directing his view
To find out men's virtues, and finding them few,
Quite sick of pursuing each troublesome elf,
He grew lazy at last, and drew from himself?
 Here Douglas retires, from his toils to relax,
The scourge of impostors, the terror of quacks.   80
Come, all ye quack bards, and ye quacking divines,
Come, and dance on the spot where your tyrant reclines!
When satire and censure encircled his throne,
I fear'd for your safety, I fear'd for my own;
But now he is gone, and we want a detector,
Our Dodds shall be pious, our Kenricks shall lecture,
Macpherson write bombast, and call it a style,
Our Townshend make speeches, and I shall compile;
New Lauders and Bowers the Tweed shall cross over,
No countryman living their tricks to discover;   90
Detection her taper shall quench to a spark,
And Scotchman meet Scotchman, and cheat in the dark.

Here lies David Garrick, describe me who can,
An abridgment of all that was pleasant in man:
As an actor, confess'd without rival to shine;
As a wit, if not first, in the very first line;
Yet, with talents like these, and an excellent heart,
The man had his failings, a dupe to his art.
Like an ill-judging beauty, his colours he spread
And beplaster'd with rouge his own natural red.   100
On the stage he was natural, simple, affecting;
'Twas only that when he was off he was acting.
With no reason on earth to go out of his way,
He turn'd and he varied full ten times a day.
Though secure of our hearts, yet confoundedly sick
If they were not his own by finessing and trick:
He cast off his friends, as a huntsman his pack,
For he knew when he pleas'd he could whistle them back.
Of praise a mere glutton, he swallow'd what came,
And the puff of a dunce he mistook it for fame;   110
Till his relish grown callous, almost to disease,
Who pepper'd the highest was surest to please.
But let us be candid, and speak out our mind,
If dunces applauded, he paid them in kind.
Ye Kenricks, ye Kellys, ye Woodfalls so grave,
What a commerce was yours while you got and you gave,
How did Grub-street re-echo the shouts that vou rais'd,
While he was be-Roscius'd, and you were beprais'd!
But peace to his spirit, wherever it flies,
To act as an angel, and mix with the skies: 120
Those poets, who owe their best fame to his skill,
Shall still be his flatterers, go where he will;
Old Shakespeare receive him with praise and with love,
And Beaumonts and Bens be his Kellys above.

    Here Hickey reclines, a most blunt, pleasant creature,
And slander itself must allow him good-nature;
He cherish'd his friend, and he relish'd a bumper;

Yet one fault he had, and that one was a thumper.
Perhaps you may ask if the man was a miser?
I answer, no, no—for he always was wiser.   '30
Too courteous, perhaps, or obligingly flat?
His very worst foe can't accuse him of that.
Perhaps he confided in men as they go,
And so was too foolishly honest? Ah, no!
Then what was his failing? come, tell it, and burn ye!
He was—could he help it?—a special attorney.
   Here Reynolds is laid, and, to tell you my mind,
He has not left a wiser or better behind:

His pencil was striking, resistless, and grand;
His manners were gentle, complying, and bland;   140
Still born to improve us in every part,
His pencil our faces, his manners our heart.
To coxcombs averse, yet most civilly steering,
When they judg'd without skill he was still hard of hearing;
When they talk'd of their Raphaels, Correggios, and stuff,
He shifted his trumpet, and only took snuff.
By flattery unspoil'd——

POSTSCRIPT.

HERE Whitefoord reclines, and deny it who can,
Though he *merrily* liv'd, he is now a *grave* man.
Rare compound of oddity, frolic, and fun!
Who relish'd a joke, and rejoic'd in a pun;
Whose temper was generous, open, sincere;
A stranger to flattery, a stranger to fear;
Who scatter'd around wit and humour at will;
Whose daily *bons mots* half a column might fill;
A Scotchman, from pride and from prejudice free;
A scholar, yet surely no pedant was he.   10

What pity, alas! that so liberal a mind
Should so long be to newspaper essays confin'd;
Who perhaps to the summit of science could soar,
Yet content "if the table he set on a roar;"
Whose talents to fill any station were fit,
Yet happy if Woodfall confessed him a wit.

Ye newspaper witlings! ye pert scribbling folks!
Who copied his squibs and re-echo'd his jokes;
Ye tame imitators, ye servile herd, come,
Still follow your master, and visit his tomb: 20
To deck it bring with you festoons of the vine,
And copious libations bestow on his shrine;

Then strew all around it—you can do no less—
Cross-readings, ship-news, and *mistakes of the press.*
   Merry Whitefoord, farewell! for *thy* sake I admit
That a Scot may have humour—I had almost said wit:
This debt to thy memory I cannot refuse,
"Thou best-humour'd man with the worst-humour'd muse."

THE CLUB.

NOTES.

LIST OF ABBREVIATIONS.

A. S., Anglo-Saxon.
A. V., the *Authorized Version of the Bible.*
Adv. of L., Bacon's *Advancement of Learning.*
An. Nat., Goldsmith's *Animated Nature.*
Arc., Milton's *Arcades.*
C., Craik's *English of Shakespeare* (Rolfe's edition).
C. T., Chaucer's *Canterbury Tales.*
Cf. (*confer*), compare.
D. V., Goldsmith's *Deserted Village.*
Foll., following.
F. Q., Spenser's *Faërie Qu.....e.*
Fr., French.
H., Haven's *Rhetoric* (Harper's edition).
Hales, *Longer English Poems* edited by Rev. J. W. Hales (London).
P. L., Milton's *Paradise Lost*
Shakes. Gr., Abbott's *Shakespearian Grammar* (the references are to *sections*, not pages).
Shep. Kal., Spenser's *Shepherd's Kalendar.*
Trav., Goldsmith's *Traveller.*
V. of W., Goldsmith's *Vicar of Wakefield.*
Wb., Webster's Dictionary (last revised quarto edition).
Wh., Whately's *Rhetoric* (Harper's edition).
Worc., Worcester's Dictionary (quarto edition).

Other abbreviations (names of books in the Bible, plays of Shakespeare, etc.), need no explanation.

NOTES.

THE TRAVELLER.

THIS poem, as we learn from the Dedication, was begun in Switzerland in 1755, but it was not completed until 1764. It was published in December of that year, and was the earliest production to which Goldsmith prefixed his name.* Johnson introduced it to the good opinion of the public by a notice in the *Critical Review* (December, 1764). The article, which is largely made up of quotations from the poem, ends thus: "Such is the poem on which we now congratulate the public, as on a production to which, since the death of Pope, it will not be easy to find anything equal." Its success was immediate;† four editions being called for within eight months, and five more during the author's lifetime,

"The nominal object of the poem," says Mr. Hales, "is to show that, as far as happiness is concerned, one form of government is as good as another. This was a favourite paradox with Dr. Johnson. Whether he or Goldsmith really believed it, may be reasonably doubted. Of course it is true that no political arrangements, however excellent, can secure for any individual citizen immunity from misery; it is true also that different political systems may suit different peoples, and, further, that every political system has its special dangers; and it is true, again, that what constitution may be adapted for what people is often a question of the profoundest difficulty; it is true, lastly, that no civil constitution relieves any one enjoying the benefit of it from his own proper duties and re-

---

* The title-page of the first edition reads thus: "The Traveller, or a Prospect of Society. A Poem. Inscribed to the Rev. Mr. Henry Goldsmith. By Oliver Goldsmith, M B. London: Printed for J. Newbery, in St. Paul's Church-yard, MDCCLXV."

† The appearance of "The Traveller" at once altered Goldsmith's intellectual standing in the estimation of society; but its effect upon the Club, if we may judge from the account given by Hawkins, was almost ludicrous. They were lost in astonishment that a "newspaper essayist" and "bookseller's drudge" should have written such a poem. On the evening of its announcement to them Goldsmith had gone away early, after "rattling away as usual," and they knew not how to reconcile his heedless garrulity with the serene beauty, the easy grace, the sound good-sense, and the occasional elevation of his poetry. They could scarcely believe that such magic numbers had flowed from a man to whom in general, says Johnson, "it was with difficulty they could give a hearing." "Well," exclaimed Chamier, "I do believe he wrote this poem himself, and, let me tell you, that is believing a great deal."—IRVING.

sponsibilities; but it is assuredly not true that there is no relation what-
ever between the government of a country and the happiness of its in-
habitants.   A government can, as it pleases, or according to its enlight-
enment, make circumstances favourable or unfavourable to individual de-
velopment and happiness. . . . Fortunately one's enjoyment of the poem
does not depend on the accuracy of the creed it professes."

THE DEDICATION.—In the first edition the second paragraph is as
follows :

"I now perceive, my dear brother, the wisdom of your humble choice.
You have entered upon a sacred office, while you have left the field of
ambition, where the labourers are many, and the harvest not worth carry-
ing away.   But of all kinds of ambition, as things are now circumstanced,
perhaps that which pursues poetical fame is the wildest.   What from
the increased refinement of the times, from the diversity of judgments
produced by opposing systems of criticism, and from the more prevalent
divisions of opinion influenced by party, the strongest and happiest efforts
can expect to please but in a very narrow circle.   Though the poet were
as sure of his aim as the imperial archer of antiquity, who boasted that
he never missed the heart, yet would many of his shafts now fly at ran-
dom, for the heart is too often in the wrong place."

There are a few verbal variations in other parts of the Dedication, but
none worth mentioning, except, perhaps, one in the last paragraph—"that
every state has a peculiar principle of happiness ; and that this principle
in each, and in our own in particular, may be carried to a mischievous
excess."

1. *Slow.*   At the first meeting of the Literary Club after the publication
of the poem, Chamier said to Goldsmith : "What do you mean by the
last word in the first line of your 'Traveller,' 'remote, unfriended, solita-
ry, *slow ?*' do you mean tardiness of locomotion ?"—"Yes," replied Gold-
smith, inconsiderately, being probably flurried at the moment.   "No,
sir," interposed his protecting friend, Johnson, "you did not mean tardi-
ness of locomotion ; you meant that sluggishness of mind which comes
upon a man in solitude."—"Ah," exclaimed Goldsmith, "*that* was what
I meant."   Chamier immediately believed that Johnson himself had writ-
ten the line, and a rumour became prevalent that he was the author of
many of the finest passages.   This was ultimately set at rest by Johnson
himself, who marked with a pencil all the verses he had contributed, nine in
number—the 420th, and the last ten lines, except the 435th and the 436th.

3. Carinthia is a province of Austria, east of the Tyrol.   Goldsmith
visited it in 1755.

8. *Untravell'd.*   That has not travelled.   In "an untravelled path,"
etc., the word is used in its ordinary passive sense.   Cf. *learned* in "a
learned man," *well-behaved* (in *Othello,* iv. 2, we find "How have I been be-
haved ?"), *well-spoken* ("For Clarence is well-spoken," *Richard III.* i.
3), *well-read* ("a well-read man"), etc.   It seems to us that *mistaken* in
"You are mistaken," which is condemned by some of the grammar-
makers, is another example of the same kind.

10. Goldsmith has the same metaphor (H. p. 102) in the *Citizen of the World*, iii.: "The farther I travel, I feel the pain of separation with stronger force; those ties that bind me to my native country and you are still unbroken. By every remove I only drag a greater length of chain." Cf. also Cibber, *Com. Lover:* "When I am with Florimel, it [my heart] is still your prisoner, it only drags a longer chain after it."

13. Cf. *D. V.* 149–162.

15. *Want and pain.* A common form of metonymy. H. p. 78.

17. *Crown'd.* Cf. *Ps.* lxv. 11. The 1st ed. reads, "Blest be those feasts where mirth and peace abound."

23. [Of what verb is *me* the object?]

26. Cf. "A Letter from a Traveller" in *The Bee*, no. 1: "When will my restless disposition give me leave to enjoy the present hour? When at Lyons, I thought all happiness lay beyond the Alps; when in Italy, I found myself still in want of something, and expected to leave solitude behind me by going into Roumelia; and now you find me turning back, still expecting ease everywhere but where I am."

27. *Like the circle*, etc. For the mixture of metaphor and simile, see Wh. p. 198. Cf. *V. of W.* ch. xxix.: "Death, the only friend of the wretched, for a little while mocks the weary traveller with the view, and like his horizon still flies before him."

32. *I sit me down.* This reflexive use of *sit* is not unusual in our old writers, and is recognized by Wb. and Worc. Some of the grammars give it as an example of false syntax, and would make it "set me down." Cf. the French *s'asseoir.* The use of the personal pronoun for the reflexive is common in Elizabethan and earlier English. Cf. Milton, *P. L.* ix. 1121: "They sat them down to weep," etc. Hales says: "In these and all such phrases the pronoun is the ethic dative, as in 'he plucked me ope his doublet,'* etc."

33. *Above the storm's career.* Cf. *D. V.* 190.

34. *An hundred.* Cf. *D. V.* 93: "an hare." As Hales remarks, our present rule that *a* rather than *an* is to be used before a word beginning with a consonant or a sounded *h* is of comparatively modern date. In A. S. the shortened form does not occur; in mediæval writers *an* is the more common form. The distinction between the numeral and the article was not fairly established before Chaucer's day. He commonly uses *an* before *h*, as "an hare" (*C. T.* 686), "an holy man." (*Id.* 5637), etc. In the *A. V.* we have "an house" (1 *Kings* ii. 24, etc.), "an husband" (*Num.* xxx. 6, etc.), but elsewhere "a husband," "an hundred," "an host," "an hand," "a harp" (1 *Chron.* xxv. 3, but "an harp," 1 *Sam.* xvi. 16), "a hammer" (*Jer.* xxiii. 29, but "an hammer," *Judg.* iv. 21), "a high wall," "an high hand," etc. Shakespeare's usage is pretty much the same as that of our day; as "a hawk, a horse, or a husband" (*Much Ado*, iii. 4), "a hare" (1 *Hen. IV.* i. 3), etc.

38. The first ed. reads as follows:

---

* Shakes. *J. C.* i 2. Here, as in *Mer. of Ven.* i. 3, "The skilful shepherd pill'd me certain wands," the *me* is clearly expletive (like the Latin "ethical dative"), but "sit me down" seems to us a different construction. Abbott recognizes both in his *Shakes. Gr.* See §§ 220, 223.

> "Amidst the store 'twere thankless to repine.
> 'Twere affectation all, and school-taught pride,
> To spurn the splendid things by Heaven supply'd.
> Let school-taught pride," etc.

41. *School-taught pride.* The pride which the Stoic felt in his conquest of himself and in his superiority to the casualties of life.

42. *These little things.* Those which "make each humbler bosom vain."

45–49. See lines 34–36. For the figures see H. pp. 153, 156.

48. *Ye bending swains.* Stooping to their work. *Swain* was, as Hales remarks, "the poet's word for *peasant* in the last century." It is by no means rare in earlier writers (Shakespeare uses it some twenty-five times), but in Goldsmith's day it had to do duty on all occasions. On *dress* cf. *Gen.* ii. 11.

50. This is the reading of the 1st and of all the modern editions, but some of the earlier ones (the 13th among them) have "Creation's tenant, all the world is mine."

52. *Recounts.* In its literal sense of "counts again."

57. *Prevails.* That is, "will out." *Sorrows fall* may mean, "fall upon or oppress the heart;" or possibly *sorrows* = "signs of sorrow, *i. e.* tears," as Hales explains it.

58. [*To see.* Would this use of the infinitive be allowable in prose? Cf. *Shakes. Gr.* 356.] The 1st ed. has "sum of human bliss."

60. *Consigned.* Assigned, appropriated.

66. The 1st ed. reads, "Boldly asserts that country for his own;" and in 68, "And live-long nights," etc.

69. *The line.* The equator.

70. *Palmy wine.* Liquor made from the sap of the palm.

73. The 1st ed. has "Nor less the patriot's boast," etc.

75, foll. The 1st ed. reads thus:

> "And yet, perhaps, if states with states we scan,
> Or estimate their bliss on Reason's plan,
> Though patriots flatter, and though fools contend,
> We still shall find uncertainty suspend,
> Find that each good, by Art or Nature given,
> To these or those, but makes the balance even:
> Find that the bliss of all is much the same,
> And patriotic boasting reason's shame."

Bliss, by the way, is a pet word with Goldsmith.

77. [What difference in the meaning would *will,* instead of *shall,* make?]

79, 80. The pointing is according to the early editions. The lines are often printed thus:

> "As different good, by Art or Nature given
> To different nations, makes their blessings even."

83. *With food,* etc. This couplet is not found in the 1st ed.

84. *Idra's cliffs.* Idria is a town among the mountains of Carniola, 1542 feet above the sea. The neighbourhood is famous for its quicksilver mines.

Arno's shelvy side. That is, its gently sloping side. Cf. *Merry Wives,* iii. 5 : "I had been drowned, but that the shore was shelvy and shallow."

85. *Rocky crested.* Virtually one word, and sometimes printed with the hyphen. In the 1st ed. this line reads, "And though rough rocks or gloomy summits frown."

87. *Art.* Used in its wider sense, in antithesis to "Nature" (81). In 146 and 304 *arts* = the fine arts.

89. *Strong.* The adjective used adverbially, as often in poetry.

90. *Either.* The word properly means only "one of *two*," but is often used carelessly as here, even by good writers. Bacon (quoted by Johnson) has "either of the three." Cf. 1 *Kings* xviii. 27, and *neither* in *Rom.* viii. 38.. See also quotation from Addison below (129). In the present passage, as Hales suggests, "perhaps *either* may be justified by supposing the 'blessings' just enumerated to be considered as divided in a twofold manner : (i.) the one prevailing ; (ii.) the others, which are cast into the shade by that prevailing one."

91. *Where wealth,* etc. This couplet is not in the 1st ed.

92. *And honour sinks.* Wordsworth, in one of his *Sonnets,* says :

"Ennobling thoughts depart
When men change swords for ledgers, and desert
The student's bower for gold."

98. *Peculiar pain.* Its proper pain, or that peculiar to itself. Cf. Gray, *Ode on the Pleasure arising from Vicissitude :*

"Still where rosy pleasure leads
See a kindred grief pursue."

101. *My proper cares.* My personal cares.

105. *Apennine.* The singular poetically used for the plural.

108. *In gay theatric pride.* "The stage often borrows similes and metaphors from nature ; here nature is made indebted to the stage !" (Hales). Cf. Virgil, *Æn.* i. 164 : "Silvis scaena coruscis ;" and *Æn.* v. 288 :

—"quem collibus undique curvis
Cingebant silvae, mediaque in valle theatri
Circus erat ;"

also Seneca, *Troades,* 1125 : "Crescit more theatri."

111. Cf. Virgil's panegyric on Italy, *Geo.* ii. 136–176.

118. *Vernal lives.* Short as the spring.

121. *Gelid.* Not a common word in English poetry. Thomson (*Summer*) has "gelid founts," and (*Autumn*) "gelid pores." It is not found in Shakes. (though he quotes the Latin "gelidus timor" in 2 *Hen. VI.* iv. 1, and "gelida umbra" in *L. L. L.* iv. 2), or Milton, or Tennyson.

122. *To winnow fragrance.* To waft, or diffuse it.

123. *Sense.* The senses.

124. The 1st and 13th eds. read, "all this nation knows ;" and two lines below, "Men seem."

127. *Manners.* In the sense of the Latin *mores.* Cf. Wordsworth, *Sonnet to Milton :*

"And give us manners, virtue, freedom, power."

128. For the figure see H. p. 118.

129. *Zealous.* In a religious sense. Cf. Addison, *Spectator,* no. 185 : "I would have every zealous man examine his heart thoroughly, and I

H

believe he will often find that what he calls a zeal for his religion is either
pride, interest, or ill-nature."

133. *Not far removed the date.* The 1st and 13th, and some modern
editions, have "nor far removed." Venice, Florence, Genoa, and Pisa
attained their commercial prime in the 15th century.

136. *Long-fallen.* That is, since the old Roman days. We need not
give a list of the Italian architects, painters, and sculptors alluded to in
these lines.

139. "Two of the main causes, certainly, of the decay of Italian com-
merce were the discovery of America and that of the sea-route to India"
(Hales).

140. The 1st and 13th eds. read, "Soon Commerce turn'd on other
shores her sail." The next two lines are not in the 1st ed.

143. *Skill.* In the old sense of knowledge. It was also used as a
verb = know, understand. See 1 *Kings* v. 6; 2 *Chron.* ii. 7, 8, and xxxiv.
12. Bacon (*Adv. of L.* i. 7, 12) translates "Sullam nescisse litteras" by
"Sylla could not skill of letters."

144. Cf. *D. V.* 389–394; also *Cit. of World,* i. : "In short, the state re-
sembled one of those bodies bloated with disease, whose bulk is only a
symptom of its wretchedness; their former opulence only rendered them
more impotent."

145. The 1st ed. reads as follows :

> "Yet though to fortune lost, here still abide
> Some splendid arts, the wrecks of former pride;
> From which the feeble heart," etc.

150. Cf. *Pres. State of Learning:* "Where, in the midst of porticos,
processions, and cavalcades, abbés turn shepherds ; and shepherdesses,
without sheep, indulge their innocent *divertimenti.*"

153. Irving (p. 160) says : "We hear much about 'poetic inspiration,'
and the 'poet's eye in a fine phrensy rolling;' but Sir Joshua Reynolds
gives an anecdote of Goldsmith while engaged upon his poem, calculated
to cure our notions about the ardour of composition. Calling upon the
poet one day, he opened the door without ceremony, and found him in
the double occupation of turning a couplet and teaching a pet dog to sit
upon his haunches. At one time he would glance his eye at his desk,
and at another shake his finger at the dog to make him retain his posi-
tion. The last lines on the page were still wet; they form part of the
description of Italy :

> 'By sports like these are all their cares beguiled,
> The sports of children satisfy the child.'

Goldsmith, with his usual good-humour, joined in the laugh caused by
his whimsical employment, and acknowledged that his boyish sport with
the dog suggested the stanza."

After the 154th line, the 1st ed. reads,

> "At sports like these, while foreign arms advance,
> In passive ease they leave the world to chance.
> When struggling Virtue sinks by long controul,
> She leaves at last, or feebly mans the soul ;"

The 13th ed. reads thus :

> "At Sports like these when foreign Arms advance,
> In passive Ease they leave the World to Chance.
> When noble Aims have suffer'd long Controul,
> They sink at last, or feebly man the Soul.
> When low Delights," etc.

156. *Feebly mans the soul.* The metaphor of a vessel is continued in this expression.

159. *Domes.* In its familiar poetic sense (its original one, by the way, from Latin *domus*) of house, mansion, palace, etc. Cf. *D. V.* 319.

167. *Bleak.* Transferred, by metonymy, from the country to its inhabitants. The word (akin to *bleach*) originally meant pale, and was applied to persons. *Mansions* is the original reading, though *mansion* (which is Masson's reading in the *Globe* ed.) would be better—in its literal sense (Latin *manere*) of an abiding-place.

In this description of Switzerland it will be observed that there is no appreciation of the wild beauty and grandeur of the scenery which attract the throngs of tourists in our day. Cf. Macaulay, *Hist. of Eng.* chap. 13 : " Goldsmith was one of the very few Saxons who, more than a century ago, ventured to explore the Highlands. He was disgusted by the hideous wilderness, and declared that he greatly preferred the charming country round Leyden, the vast expanse of verdant meadow, and the villas with their statues and grottoes, trim flower-beds and rectilinear avenues. Yet it is difficult to believe that the author of *The Traveller* and *The Deserted Village* was naturally inferior in taste and sensibility to the thousands of clerks and milliners who are now thrown into raptures by the sight of Loch Katrine and Loch Lomond."

Cf. also what Ruskin (*Modern Painters*, vol. iii.) says of the Greeks— their "fear of all that was disorderly, unbalanced, and rugged;" that "every Homeric landscape, intended to be beautiful, is composed of a fountain, a meadow, and a shady grove;" and again of "the mediæval mind as agreeing wholly with the ancients, in holding that flat land, brooks, and groves of aspens compose the pleasant places of the earth, and that rocks and mountains are, for inhabitation, altogether to be reprobated and detested." Of the *Divina Commedia* he says: "In no part of the poem do we find allusion to mountains in any other than a stern light ; nor the slightest evidence that Dante cared to look at them. From that hill of San Miniato, whose steps he knew so well, the eye commands, at the farther extremity of the Val d'Arno, the whole purple range of the mountains of Carrara, peaked and mighty, seen always against the sunset light in silent outline, the chief forms that rule the scene as twilight fades away. By this vision Dante seems to have been wholly unmoved, and, but for Lucan's mention of Aruns at Luna, would seemingly not have spoken of the Carrara hills in the whole course of his poem : when he does allude to them, he speaks of their white marble, and their command of stars and sea, but has evidently no regard for the hills themselves."

168. The line forcibly expresses the labour required to wring, as it were, from the soil its scanty produce.

169, 170. One might infer at first that the poet meant that Switzerland furnished iron as well as mercenary soldiers; but there are no iron mines in the country. It had furnished the soldiers from the 15th century. Cf. *Hamlet*, iv. 5 : "Where are my Switzers?"

176. *Redress the clime.* Make amends for it. Cf. 214, where *redrest* means relieved, or supplied. It originally meant to put in order again, to set right. Cf. Milton, *P. L.* ix. 219 :

> "While I,
> In yonder spring of roses intermixt
> With myrtle, find what to redress till noon."

178. *He sees*, etc. Cf. Cæsar, *B. G.* vi. : "Cum suas quisque opes cum potentissimis aequari videat."

186. *Breasts.* This is the reading of all the early editions, and Johnson quotes it in his *Dict.* as an illustration of the verb. The reading "Breathes," found in the *Globe* ed. and some others, doubtless had its origin in a misprint.

187. *The finny deep.* Cf. *Cit. of World*, ii. : "The best manner to draw up the finny prey." On the transfer of the adjective, cf. 167, and *D. V.* 361 : "the warbling grove." In "patient angle" and "venturous ploughshare" we have a similar figure.

190. *Savage.* Rarely used as a noun except of human beings. Pope (*Iliad*, xviii. 373) applies it to a lion :

> "When the grim savage, to his rifled den
> Too late returning, snuffs the track of men."

Goldsmith uses it in the same sense in prose, as in *Cit. of World*, i. : "drive the reluctant savage into the toils."

191. *Sped.* Accomplished. The verb *speed*, in this sense, means simply to carry through successfully, with no special reference to quickness. Cf. *Judges* v. 30. The noun *speed* in "I wish you good speed" (of which "God speed" is probably a corruption) is similarly used = success. Cf. *Gen.* xxiv. 12 with 2 *John* 10, 11.

197. Cf. *D. V.* 155–160. *Nightly* = for the night; not, as usual, for a succession of nights. Cf. Milton, *Il Pens.* 84 : "To bless the doors from nightly harm;" *Arc.* 48, etc. So often in Shakes.

201. The 13th ed. has "And even those Hills."

203. *Conforms.* Suits itself.

205. *And as a child.* The 1st and 13th eds. have "as a babe."

206. *Close and closer.* "Perhaps = closer and closer; but the former comparative inflection is omitted for euphony's and the metre's sake, just as one adverbial inflection is omitted in 'safe and nicely,' *Lear*, v. 3" (Hales). Cf. the omission of the superlative inflection in "the generous and gravest citizens" (*M. for M.* iv. 6), "the soft and sweetest music" (Ben Jonson), "only the grave and wisest of the land" (Heywood), etc. See *Shakes. Gr.* 397, 398.

213. The 1st ed. has "Since every want." Cf. *An. Nat.* ii. : "Every want becomes a means of pleasure in the redressing."

216. *Supplies.* Satisfies.

219, 220. [Is there a confusion of metaphors here?]

221. *Level.* Unvaried, monotonous. Cf. 359. Mrs. Browning, in one of her *Sonnets*, says : "We miss far prospects by a level bliss."

222. The 1st and 13th eds. read, "Nor quench'd by want, nor fan'd [*sic*] by strong desire."

226. [How is the form *expire* to be justified?]

232. *Fall* is not grammatically correct, but may be explained as an instance of "construction according to sense."

233. A good example of the mixture of metaphor and simile. Wh. p. 198.

234. *Cowering.* Simply, brooding, with no notion of fear. Cf. Dryden: "Our dame sits cowering o'er a kitchen fire." The verb was also used transitively, as in Spenser, *F. Q.* ii. 8, 9 :

> "He much rejoyst, and courd it tenderly,
> As chicken newly hatcht, from dreaded destiny;"

that is, shielded or protected it, as a bird does its young.

243. Cf. the narrative of the "philosophic vagabond" in the *Vicar of Wakefield*: "I had some knowledge of music, with a tolerable voice; I now turned what was once my amusement into a present means of subsistence. I passed among the harmless peasants of Flanders, and among such of the French as were poor enough to be very merry, for I ever found them sprightly in proportion to their wants. Whenever I approached a peasant's house towards nightfall, I played one of my merriest tunes, and that procured me not only a lodging, but subsistence for the next day; but in truth I must own, whenever I attempted to enter-

tain persons of a higher rank, they always thought my performance odious, and never made me any return for my endeavours to please them."

244. *Tuneless.* Explained by 247, 248 below.

253. *Gestic lore.* Some explain this as "legendary lore." See Wb. *s. v.* But it seems more natural to refer it to his skill in dancing. Cf. Scott, *Peveril of the Peak,* ch. xxx. : "He seemed, like herself, carried away by the enthusiasm of the gestic art."

255. The 13th ed. has "So bright a Life."

256. *Idly busy.* The rhetorical figure called "oxymoron." Cf. Horace's "Strenua nos exercet inertia," and Pope's (*Elegy on an Unfortunate Lady*)

> "Life's idle business at one gasp be o'er."

Rolls their world away. Cf. *Hamlet,* iii. 2 : "Thus runs the world away."

264. *An avarice of praise.* Cf. Horace, *Ars Poetica,* 324 : "Praeter laudem nullius avaris."

265, 266. See p. 38, foot-note.

273. *Tawdry.* Said to be derived from St. Audrey (St. Ethelreda), at the fairs held on whose days toys and finery, especially laces, were sold. Originally the word had no depreciatory sense. Cf. Shakes. *W. T.* iv. 3 : "Come, you promised me a tawdry lace and a pair of sweet gloves;" and Spenser, *Shep. Kal. Apr. :*

> "Binde your fillets faste,
> And gird in your waste,
> For more finenesse, with a tawdrie lace."

The word was also used as a noun, meaning a rustic necklace. Cf. Drayton, *Polyolbion,* ii. :

> "Of which the Naiads and the blue Nereids make
> Them taudries for their necks."

276. *Frieze.* A coarse woollen cloth. Cf. Milton. *Comus,* 722 : "Drink the clear stream, and nothing wear but frieze."

277. *Cheer.* Fare. For the successive meanings of this word, which originally meant the face (Fr. *chère*), see Wb. or C. p. 278.

280. Cf. Pope, *Essay on Man,* iv. 255 :

> "One self-approving hour whole years outweighs
> Of stupid starers and of loud huzzas."

281. Cf. what Goldsmith says of Holland in one of his letters : "Nothing can equal its beauty; wherever I turn my eyes, fine houses, elegant gardens, statues, grottoes, vistas, present themselves ; but when you enter their towns you are charmed beyond description. No misery is to be seen here ; every one is usefully employed."

283. *Methinks.* In this word *me* is the dative and *thinks* (the A. S. *thincan,* to seem, not *thencan,* to think) is impersonal. In Chaucer we find *him thoughte, hem* (them) *thoughte,* etc.; also, *it thinketh me,* etc.

284. *Leans against the land.* Cf. Dryden, *Annus Mirabilis,* st. 164 :

> "And view the ocean leaning on the sky;"

also Statius, *Theb.* iv. 62 : "Et terris maria inclinata repellit."

286. *Rampire.* The same word as *rampart.* It was also used as a verb. Cf. Shakes. *T. of A.* v. 5 : " Our rampired gates." The 13th ed. has " Rampart's " here, and two lines below both the 1st and 13th have " seems to go."

289. *Spreads its long arms,* etc. In the 1st ed. this couplet begins, " That spreads its arms," and follows 286, which ends with a comma. 287 and 288 follow 290, and 291 reads, " While ocean pent and rising o'er the pile."

291. In the *Animated Nature,* Goldsmith says : " The whole kingdom of Holland seems to be a conquest on the sea, and in a manner rescued from its bosom. The surface of the earth in this country is below the level of the bed of the sea ; and I remember upon approaching the coast to have looked down upon it from the sea as into a valley."

297. *Wave-subjected.* Lying below the level of the waves ; or, perhaps, as some explain it, " exposed to the inroads of the waves."

303. *Are.* The plural is grammatically incorrect ; but see on 232.

305. Cf. *V. of W.* ch. xix. : " Now the possessor of accumulated wealth, when furnished with the necessaries and pleasures of life, has no other method to employ the superfluity of his fortune but in purchasing power ; that is, differently speaking, in making dependants, by purchasing the liberty of the needy or the venal, of men who are willing to bear the mortification of contiguous tyranny for bread."

309. This line occurs verbatim in the *Citizen of the World,* i. : " A nation once famous for setting the world an example of freedom is now become a land of tyrants and a den of slaves."

311. *Calmly bent.* Tamely stooping to the yoke.

312. The 1st and 13th eds. read, " Dull as their lakes that sleep beneath the storm."

313. In an Introduction to the *Hist. of the Seven Years' War,* Goldsmith says : " How unlike the brave peasants, their ancestors, who spread terror in India, and always declared themselves the allies of those who drew the sword in defence of freedom !"

316. " In the 16th century they had fought stoutly against the same domineering enemy as England had withstood ; in the 17th they had contested with England the queenship of the seas " (Hales).

319. *Lawns.* Cf. *D. V.* 35. " Arcadia, perhaps most noted in the Greek and Latin writers for the stupidity of its inhabitants, was about the time of the revival of learning adopted as the ideal of rural beauty " (Hales). *Arcadici sensus, Arcadicae aures,* etc., were proverbial synonyms for " pastoral dulness," and *Arcadicus juvenis* in Juvenal (vii. 160) is equivalent to blockhead ; but see Virgil, *Ecl.* vii. 4 ; x. 30.

320. *Hydaspes.* One of the tributaries of the Indus, now known as the Jelum, or Jhelum. Its Sanscrit name was Vitastâ, of which Hydaspes is a corruption. Horace (*Od.* i. 22, 8) calls it " fabulosus," from the marvellous tales connected with it.

324. That is, the extremes of climate are known there only in imagination.

327. *Port.* Cf. Gray's *Bard,* 117 : " Her lion port, her awe-commanding face."

328. In the 1st ed. this line precedes 327.

330. Cf. Tennyson, *Locksley Hall:* "Cursed be the sickly forms that err from honest nature's rule !"

332. *Imagined right.* What he believes to be his right.

333. *Boasts these rights to scan.* "Boasts that he scans these rights, that he takes his part in the discussion of public questions" (Hales).

341. This line and the next are not in the 1st ed. In 342 the 13th ed. has "All kindred Claims that soften Life unknown." In the 1st ed. 343 reads, "See, though by circling deeps together held." In 350 both eds. have "As social bonds decay."

345. *Ferments.* Political agitations. *Imprisoned* = "restrained within the bounds of law."

351. *Fictitious.* Factitious, artificial.

357. *Stems.* Families. The 13th ed. has "patriot claim;" and in both the 1st and 13th the next line reads, "And monarchs toil, and poets pant for fame."

358. *Wrote.* For *written.* Cf. *Lear,* i. 2 : "he hath wrote this ;" *Cymb.* iii. 5 : "Lucius hath wrote already to the emperor ;" *A. and C.* iii. 5 : "letters he had formerly wrote ;" but *writ* is the usual form of the participle in Shakes. The latter is the curtailed form of *written,* and these curtailed forms (*spoke, broke, forgot, chid, froze,* etc.) are common in the Elizabethan writers. See *Shakes. Gr.* 343.

362. *The great.* "This was a very favorite phrase about Goldsmith's time" (Hales). After this line the 1st ed. has the couplet,

> "Perish the wish; for inly satisfied,
> Above their pomps I hold my ragged pride."

Lines 363-380 are not in 1st ed.

363. *Ye powers,* etc. Cf. Pope, *Elegy on an Unfortunate Lady:*

> "Why bade ye else, ye powers, her soul aspire
> Beyond the vulgar flights of low desire?"

365. "The literature of the last century abounds with apostrophes to Liberty. That theme was the great commonplace of the time. Goldsmith has his laugh at it in the *Vicar of Wakefield,* ch. xix." (Hales).

369. *Blooms.* Cf. 115.

372. Cf. Thomson, *Summer :*

> "While thus laborious crowds
> Ply the tough oar, philosophy directs
> The ruling helm."

The 13th ed. reads, "That those who think most, govern those that Toil."

374. The 13th ed. reads,

> "proportion'd Loads on each ;
> Much on the Low, the Rest, as Rank supplies,
> Should in columnar Diminution rise ;
> While, should one Order," etc.

We have found this couplet ("Much on," etc.) nowhere else, and it is mentioned by none of the editors.

378. *Who think.* That is, are they who think.

380. *Warms.* That is, "my soul."

382. *Contracting regal power.* In the preface to the *Hist. of England,*

Goldsmith says : "It is not yet decided in politics whether the diminution of kingly power in England tends to increase the happiness or freedom of the people. For my own part, from seeing the bad effects of the tyranny of the great in those republican states that pretend to be free, I cannot help wishing that our monarchs may still be allowed to enjoy the power of controlling the encroachments of the great at home." Cf. *V. of W.* ch. xix. : "It is the interest of the great to diminish kingly power as much as possible."

386. The 13th and some other eds. read, "Law grinds the poor." Cf. *V. of W.* ch. xix. : "What they may then expect may be seen by turning our eyes to Holland, Genoa, or Venice, where the laws govern the poor, and the rich govern the law."

391. Cf. the conclusion of the vicar's harangue, *V. of W.* ch. xix.

391. *Petty tyrants.* Cf. Pope, *Ep. to Mrs. Blount :* "Marriage may all these petty tyrants chase."

396. *Gave wealth,* etc. Gave to wealth the power of swaying, etc.

397, foll. Cf. *D. V.* 49–56, 63–66, 275–282, 362–384.

411. *Oswego.* The river of that name in New York. Cf. Goldsmith's *Threnodia Augustalis :*

"Oswego's dreary shores shall be my grave."

412. *Niagara.* The accent was originally on the penult, as here. See *Lippincott's Gazetteer.*

414, 415. Cf. *D. V.,* 349–355. See also *Animated Nature :* "Where man in his savage state owns inferior strength, and the beasts claim divided dominion."

416. The 1st and 13th eds. have "And the brown Indian takes a deadly aim."

420. This line was written by Dr. Johnson. See above, on 1.

421. The 1st and 13th eds. read "Casts a fond look."

426. Cf. Pope, *Essay on Man :*

"For forms of government let fools contest;
Whate'er is best administer'd is best."

431. Cf. Milton, *P. L.* i. 254 :

"The mind is its own place, and in itself
Can make a heaven of hell, a hell of heaven."

435. Cf. Blackmore, *Eliza :* "Some the sharp axe, and some the painful wheel."

436. *Luke's iron crown.* George and Luke Dosa were two brothers who headed a revolt against the Hungarian nobles in 1514 ; and George, not Luke, underwent the torture of the red-hot iron crown as a punishment for allowing himself to be proclaimed King of Hungary by the rebels. The brothers belonged to one of the native races of Transylvania, called Szeklers (properly Székelys) or "Zecklers." Boswell (*Life of Johnson,* ch. xix.) gives "Zeck" as the name of the brothers, and Corney in his edition of Goldsmith "corrects" the text here into "*Zeck's* iron crown."

Robert François Damiens was put to death with frightful tortures in 1757 for an attempt to assassinate Louis XV. of France.

THE DESERTED VILLAGE.

THIS poem was first published in 1770. "This day at 12," said the *Public Advertiser* of May 26th of that year, "will be published, price two shillings, the *Deserted Village*, a Poem. By Doctor Goldsmith. Printed for W. Griffin, at Garrick's Head in Catherine Street, Strand." A 2d edition appeared June 7th; a 3d, June 14th; a 4th, carefully revised, June 28; and a 5th, August 16th.

The poet Gray, then passing the last summer of his life at Malvern, after hearing the poem read to him by his friend Nicholls, exclaimed, "This man is a poet."

Soon after the publication of the poem, the following verses were addressed to the author by Miss Aiken, afterwards Mrs. Barbauld:

> "In vain fair Auburn weeps her desert plains;
> She moves our envy who so well complains:
> In vain hath proud oppression laid her low;
> She wears a garland on her faded brow.
> Now, Auburn, now, absolve impartial Fate,
> Which, if it makes thee wretched, makes thee great.
> So unobserv'd, some humble plant may bloom.
> 'Till crush'd, it fills the air with sweet perfume:
> So had thy swains in ease and plenty slept,
> The Poet had not sung, nor Britain wept.
> Nor let Britannia mourn her drooping bay,
> Unhonour'd Genius, and her swift decay:
> O Patron of the Poor! it cannot be,
> While one—one poet yet remains like thee.
> Nor can the Muse desert our favour'd isle,
> Till thou desert the Muse, and scorn her smile."

Sir Walter Scott, in the *Quarterly Review*, vol. iv., thus writes:

"It would be difficult to point out one among the English poets less likely to be excelled in his own style than the author of the *Deserted Village*. Possessing much of Pope's versification without the monotonous structure of his lines; rising sometimes to the swell and fulness of Dryden, without his inflations; delicate and masterly in his descriptions; graceful in one of the greatest graces of poetry, its transitions; alike successful in his sportive or grave, his playful or melancholy mood; he may long bid defiance to the numerous competitors whom the friendship or flattery of the present age is so hastily arraying against him."

And, again:

"The wreath of Goldsmith is unsullied: he wrote to exalt virtue and expose vice; and he accomplished his task in a manner which raises him to the highest rank among British authors. We close this volume with a sigh that such an author should have written so little from the stores of his own genius, and that he should have been so prematurely removed from the sphere of literature which he so highly adorned."

Goethe, in his *Memoirs*, refers to the poem as follows :

" A poetical production, which our little circle hailed with transport, now occupied our attention ; this was Goldsmith's *Deserted Village.* This poem seemed perfectly adapted to the sentiments which then actuated us. The pictures which it represented were those which we loved to contemplate, and sought with avidity, in order to enjoy them with all the zest of youth. Village fêtes, wakes, and fairs, the grave meetings of the elders under the village trees, to which they have retreated in order to leave the young to the pleasures of the dance ; the part taken by persons of a more elevated rank in these village entertainments ; the decency maintained in the midst of the general hilarity by a worthy clergyman, skilled to moderate mirth when approaching to boisterousness, and to prevent all that might produce discord ;—such were the representations the poet laid before us, not as the object of present attention and enjoyment, but as past pleasures, the loss of which excited regret. We found ourselves once more in our beloved Wakefield, amidst its well-known circle. But those interesting characters had now lost all life and movement ; they appeared only like shadows called up by the plaintive tones of the elegiac muse. The idea of this poem seems singularly happy to those who can enter into the author's intention, and who, like him, find a melancholy satisfaction in recalling innocent pleasures long since fled. I shared all Gotter's enthusiasm for this charming production. We both undertook to translate it ; but he succeeded better than I did, because I had too scrupulously endeavoured to transfer the tender and affecting character of the original into our language."

Irving says : " We shall not dwell upon the peculiar merits of this poem ; we cannot help noticing, however, how truly it is a mirror of the author's heart, and of all the fond pictures of early friends and early life forever present there. It seems to us as if the very last accounts received from home, of his 'shattered family,' and the desolation that seemed to have settled upon the haunts of his childhood, had cut to the roots one feebly cherished hope, and produced the following exquisitely tender and mournful lines :

> ' In all my wanderings round this world of care,
> In all my griefs—and God has given my share—
> I still had hopes, my latest hours to crown,
> Amidst these humble bowers to lay me down ;
> To husband out life's taper at the close,
> And keep the flame from wasting by repose ;
> I still had hopes, for pride attends us still,
> Amidst the swains to show my book-learn'd skill,
> Around my fire an evening group to draw,
> And tell of all I felt, and all I saw ;
> And as an hare whom hounds and horns pursue,
> Pants to the place from whence at first she flew,
> I still had hopes, my long vexations past,
> Here to return—*and die at home at last.*'

" How touchingly expressive are the succeeding lines, wrung from a heart which all the trials and temptations and buffetings of the world could not render worldly; which, amid a thousand follies and errors of the head, still retained its childlike innocence; and which, doomed to struggle on to the last amidst the din and turmoil of the metropolis, had ever been cheating itself with a dream of rural quiet and seclusion :

> 'O blest retirement, friend to life's decline,
> Retreats from care, *that never must be mine!*
> How blest is he who crowns, in shades like these,
> A youth of labour with an age of ease;
> Who quits a world where strong temptations try,
> And, since 'tis hard to combat, learns to fly!
> For him no wretches, born to work and weep,
> Explore the mine or tempt the dangerous deep;
> No surly porter stands, in guilty state,
> To spurn imploring famine from the gate ;
> But on he moves, to meet his latter end,
> Angels around befriending virtue's friend;
> Bends to the grave with unperceived decay,
> While resignation gently slopes the way;
> And, all his prospects brightening to the last,
> His heaven commences ere the world be past.' "

Mr. Hales remarks : "Goldsmith's was the one poetical voice of that time. No other poems besides his, published between Gray's *Odes* and Cowper's *Table Talk*, can be said to have lived. It is no wonder *The Deserted Village* was so widely popular. The heart of the people was not dead, though somewhat chill and cold. It warmed towards a presence so genial, so graceful, so tender.

"Here, as in his other poem, Goldsmith entertained not only an artistic, but also a didactic purpose. He wished to set forth the evils of the Luxury that was prevailing more and more widely in his day. This is a thrice old theme; but indeed what theme is not so? No doubt the vast growth of our commerce and increase of wealth in the middle and latter part of the last century especially suggested it in Goldsmith's time. Possibly enough in handling it Goldsmith made some blunders; the work could scarcely be his, if it were free from blunders. . . . He was wrong in his belief that England was at the time rapidly depopulating. . . . He was obviously wrong in ascribing this supposed depopulation to the great commercial prosperity of the time. Whatever sentimental, whatever real objections may be urged against Trade, it cannot be denied that it multiplies and widens fields of labour, and so creates populations. . . . Goldsmith's fallacy lies in identifying Trade and Luxury. . . . Again, the picture drawn of the emigrants in their new land is certainly much exaggerated. Such experience as befalls the hero of *Martin Chuzzlewit* is very much what Goldsmith conceives to await all emigrants. . . .

"But he is not always in the wrong. His attacks on Luxury, when he really means Luxury and not something else in some way associated with that cardinal pest, are well deserved and often vigorously made. And when he deplores the accumulation of land under one ownership— how 'one only master grasps the whole domain'—and how consequently the old race of small proprietors is exterminated—how 'a bold peasantry, their country's pride,' is perishing, he certainly cannot be laughed down as a maintainer of mere idle grievances. One may agree with him in his view in this matter, or one may disagree; but it cannot be denied that here he has a right to his view—that this is a question open to serious doubt and difficulty. I suppose there are few persons who will not allow there is something to regret in the almost total disappearance of the class of small freeholders, however much that something may seem to be compensated for by what has come in their place. . . . As the question is generally discussed by political economists, it lies between small farms and large farms ; . . . as it presented itself to Goldsmith, it lay between small farms and large parks—between a system of small ground-plots assiduously cultivated, and wide estates reserved for seclusion and pleasure. . . . 'Half a tillage,' as it seemed, 'stinted the smiling plain ;' and in his eyes there was no smile possible for the plain like that of the waving corn, which is, as it were, the gold-haired child of it. Then, like the gentle recluse Gray, and like the bright day-labourer Burns, he felt much sympathy with the merriments and sadnesses and interests of the common country-folk. Their life was precious to him, and he could not bear to think that the area of it was being narrowed, that for them no more the blazing hearth should burn where it had been wont, not because they were dead, but because they were ejected wanderers.

"It is from this sincere sympathy, apart from all theories and theorizings, that the force and beauty of this poem spring. When Goldsmith thinks of the decay or destruction of those scenes he prized so highly, a genuine sorrow penetrates him, and he gives it tongue as in this poem ; he becomes the loving elegist of the old yeomanry."

Mr. Forster, in his *Life and Times of Oliver Goldsmith*, comparing *The Traveller* and *The Deserted Village*, says: "All the characteristics of the first poem seem to me developed in the second ; with as chaste a simplicity, with as choice a selectness of natural expression, in verse of as musical cadence ; but with yet greater earnestness of purpose, and a far more human interest. Nor is that purpose to be lightly dismissed, because it more concerns the heart than the understanding, and is sentimental rather than philosophical. The accumulation of wealth has *not* brought about man's diminution, nor is trade's proud empire threatened with decay ; but too eager are the triumphs of both, to be always conscious of evils attendant on even the benefits they bring,—and of those it was the poet's purpose to remind us. The lesson can never be thrown away. No material prosperity can be so great, but that underneath it, and indeed because of it, will not still be found much suffering and sadness ; much to remember that is commonly forgotten, much to attend to that is almost always neglected. Trade would not thrive the less, though shortened somewhat of its unfeeling train ; nor wealth enjoy fewer blessings, if its unwieldy pomp less often spurned the cottage from the green. 'It is a melancholy thing to stand alone in one's country,' said the Lord Leicester who built Holkham, when complimented on the completion of that princely dwelling. 'I look round—not a house is to be seen but mine. I am the giant of Giant-castle, and have eat up all my neighbours.'*

---

* When asked who was his nearest neighbour, he replied, "The King of Denmark."

There is no man who has risen upward in the world, even by ways the most honourable to himself and kindly to others, who may not be said to have a deserted village, sacred to the tenderest and fondest recollections, which it is well that his fancy and his feeling should at times revisit.

"Goldsmith looked into his heart and wrote. From that great city in which his hard-spent life had been diversified with so much care and toil, he travelled back to the memory of lives more simply passed, of more cheerful labour, of less anxious care, of homely affections and humble joys for which the world and all its successes offer nothing in exchange. . . .

"Sweet Auburn is no more. But though he finds the scene deserted, for us he peoples it anew, builds up again its ruined haunts, and revives its pure enjoyments; from the glare of crowded cities, their exciting struggles and palling pleasures, carries us back to the season of natural pastimes and unsophisticated desires; adjures us all to remember, in our several smaller worlds, the vast world of humanity that breathes beyond; shows us that there is nothing too humble for the loftiest and most affecting associations; and that where human joys and interests have been, their memory is sacred forever ! . . .

"Beautifully is it said by Mr. Campbell, that ' fiction in poetry is not the reverse of truth, but her soft and enchanted resemblance; and this ideal beauty of nature has seldom been united with so much sober fidelity as in the groups and scenery of *The Deserted Village.*' It is to be added that everything in it is English, the feeling, incidents, descriptions, and allusions; and that this consideration may save us needless trouble in seeking to identify sweet Auburn (a name he obtained from Langton) with Lissoy. Scenes of the poet's youth had doubtless risen in his memory as he wrote, mingling with, and taking altered hue from, later experiences; thoughts of those early days could scarcely have been absent from the wish for a quiet close to the struggles and toil of his mature life, and very possibly, nay, almost certainly, when the dream of such a retirement haunted him, Lissoy formed part of the vision; it is even possible he may have caught the first hint of his design from a local Westmeath poet and schoolmaster,* who, in his youth, had given rhymed utterance to the old tenant grievances of the Irish rural population; nor could complaints that were also loudest in those boyish days at Lissoy, of certain reckless and unsparing evictions by which one General Naper (Napper, or Napier) had persisted in improving his estate, have passed altogether from Goldsmith's memory.† But there was nothing local in his present

---

* Lawrence Whyte, who published (1741) a poem, in whose list of subscribers appears Allan Ramsay's name, which describes with some pathos the sufferings of dispossessed Irish tenantry ·

"Their native soil were forc'd to quit,
So Irish landlords thought it fit. . . .
How many villages they razed,
How many parishes laid.waste !"

† The earliest and most intelligent attempt to identify Lissoy and Auburn was made in 1807 by Doctor Strean, Henry Goldsmith's successor in the curacy of Kilkenny West, but, at the time he wrote this letter, perpetual curate of Athlone. I quote it as the first and best outline of all that has since been very elaborately and very needlessly said on the same subject: "The poem of *The Deserted Village* took its origin from the circumstance

aim ; or if there was, it was the rustic life and rural scenery of England. It is quite natural that Irish enthusiasts should have found out the fence, the furze, the thorn, the decent church, the never-failing brook, the busy mill, even the Twelve Good Rules, and Royal Game of Goose ;* it was to be expected that pilgrims should have borne away every vestige of the first hawthorn they could lay their hands on ; it was very graceful and pretty amusement for Mr. Hogan, when he settled in the neighbourhood, to rebuild the village inn and fix the 'broken teacups' in the wall for security against the enthusiasm of predatory pilgrims, to fence round with masonry what still remained of the hawthorn, to prop up the tottering walls of what was once the parish school, and to christen his furbished-up village and adjoining mansion by the name of Auburn. All this, as

---

of General Robert Napper (the grandfather of the gentleman who now lives in the house, within half a mile of Lissoy, and built by the general) having purchased an extensive tract of the country surrounding Lissoy, or *Auburn ;* in consequence of which many families, here called cottiers, were removed, to make room for the intended improvements of what was now to become the wide domain of a rich man, warm with the idea of changing the face of his new acquisition ; and were forced, 'with fainting steps,' to go in search of 'torrid tracts' and 'distant climes.' This fact alone might be sufficient to establish the seat of the poem ; but there cannot remain a doubt in any unprejudiced mind when the following are added : viz., that the character of the village preacher, the above-named Henry, is copied from nature. He is described exactly as he lived, and his 'modest mansion' as it existed. Burn, the name of the village master, and the site of his schoolhouse ; and Catherine Giraghty, a lonely widow,

> 'The wretched matron, forc'd in age for bread
> To strip the brook with mantling cresses spread'

(and to this day the brook and ditches near the spot where her cabin stood abound with cresses), still remain in the memory of the inhabitants, and Catherine's children live in the neighbourhood. The pool, the busy mill, the house where 'nut-brown draughts inspired,' are still visited as the poetic scene ; and the 'hawthorn-bush,' growing in an open space in front of the house, which I knew to have three trunks, is now reduced to one ; the other two having been cut, from time to time, by persons carrying pieces of it away to be made into toys, etc., in honour of the bard, and of the celebrity of his poem. All these contribute to the same proof ; and the 'decent church,' which I attended for upwards of eighteen years, and which 'tops the neighbouring hill,' is exactly described as seen from Lissoy, the residence of the preacher."

* "A lady from the neighbourhood of Portglenone, in the county of Antrim, was one of those who visited the Deserted Village in the summer of 1817 ; and was fortunate enough to find, in a cottage adjoining the ale-house, an old smoked print, which she was credibly informed was the identical Twelve Good Rules which had ornamented that rural tavern, with the Royal Game of Goose, etc., etc., when Goldsmith drew his fascinating description of it."—*Gent. Mag.* vol. lxxxviii.

The "identical" old smoked print was doubtless Mr. Hogan's. "When I settled on the spot," said that gentleman, giving account of what he had done to a public meeting held in Ballymahon in 1819, to set on foot a subscription for a monument to Goldsmith's memory, "I attempted to replace some of the almost forgotten identities that delighted me forty years since. I rebuilt his Three Jolly Pigeons, restored his Twelve Good Rules and Royal Game of Goose, enclosed his Hawthorn Tree, now almost cut away by the devotion of the literary pilgrims who resort to it ; I also planted his favourite hill before Lissoy Gate," etc., etc.—*Gent. Mag.* vol. xc. The proposed monument failed, notwithstanding the honourable enthusiasm of Mr. Hogan, the Rev. John Graham, its originator, and others. I may add that soon after Mr. Hogan began his restorations, an intelligent visitor described them ; and nothing, he said, so shook his faith in the reality of Auburn as the got-up print, the fixed teacups, and so forth. But what had once been Charles and Henry Goldsmith's parsonage at Lissoy, the lower chamber of which he found inhabited by pigs and sheep, and the drawing-room by oats, was yet so placed in relation to ob-

Walter Scott has said, 'is a pleasing tribute to the poet in the land of his fathers;'* but it certainly is no more.

"Such tribute as the poem itself was, its author offered to Sir Joshua Reynolds, dedicating it to him. 'Setting interest aside,' he wrote, 'to which I never paid much attention, I must be indulged at present in following my affections. The only dedication I ever made was to my brother, because I loved him better than most other men. He is since dead. Permit me to inscribe this Poem to you.' How gratefully this was received, and how strongly it cemented an already fast friendship, needs not be said. The great painter could not rest till he had made public acknowledgment and return. He painted his picture of *Resignation*, had it engraved by Thomas Watson, and inscribed upon it these words : 'This attempt to express a character in *The Deserted Village* is dedicated to Doctor Goldsmith, by his sincere friend and admirer, Joshua Reynolds.'"

1. *Sweet Auburn.* Lissoy or Lishoy, which claims the honour of being the original Auburn (see extract from Mr. Forster above) is eight miles north of Athlone, and almost in the geographical centre of Ireland. Howitt (*Homes and Haunts of British Poets*, vol. i. p. 328, Harper's ed.) says that it now "consists of a few common cottages by the roadside, on a flat and by no means particularly interesting scene." The ruins of the house where Goldsmith's father lived are still to be seen, with "the orchard and wild remains of a garden, enclosed with a high old stone wall."

4. *Parting.* Departing, as often in poetry and in Old English. Cf. 171 : "parting life;" also Gray's *Elegy*, 1 : "parting day," and 89 : "parting soul;" Shakes. *Cor.* v. 6 : "When I parted hence," etc.; Milton, *Hymn on Nativ.* 186 : "The parting Genius," etc. On the other hand, *depart* was used in the sense of *part*. In the Marriage Service "till death us do part" is a corruption of "till death us depart." Wiclif's Bible, in *Matt.* xix. 6, has "therfor a man departe not that thing that God hath ioyned;" and Chaucer, in *Knight's Tale*, 1136, "Til that the deth departen shal us tweine."

5. *Dear lovely bowers*, etc. The ten lines beginning with this were Goldsmith's second morning's work on the poem, according to his friend Cooke, to whom he read the lines aloud. "Come," he added, "let me tell you, this is no bad morning's work; and now, my dear boy, if you are not better engaged, I should like to enjoy a shoemaker's holiday with you" (Forster).

6. Cf. Pope, *Essay on Man*, ii. :

---

jects described in the poem, as somewhat to restore his shaken belief. He adds, that, in the cabin of the quondam schoolmaster, an oak chair with a back and seat of cane, purporting to be "the chair of the poet," was shown him, apparently kept "rather for the sake of drawing contributions from the curious than from any reverence for the bard. There is," he humourously adds, "no fear of its being worn out by the devout earnestness of sitters, as the cocks and hens have usurped undisputed possession of it, and protest most clamourously against all attempts to get it cleansed, or to seat oneself."

* Colman the younger has recorded (*Random Recollections*, vol. i.) a more extraordinary tribute in the land of his adoption: "One day I met the poet Harding at Oxford, a half-crazy creature, as poets generally are, with a huge broken brick and some bits of thatch upon the crown of his hat. On my asking him for a solution of this Prosopopeia, 'Sir,' said he, 'to-day is the anniversary of the celebrated Dr. Goldsmith's death, and I am now in the character of his *Deserted Village.*'"

> "Behold the child, by nature's kindly law,
> Pleased with a rattle, tickled with a straw."

12. *Decent.* In its original sense of comely (Latin *decēns*). Cf. Milton, *Il Pens.* 36: "thy decent shoulders," etc.

16. *When toil*, etc. "When a remission of toil allowed play to have its turn."

17. *Train.* As Hales remarks, this is a frequent word in Goldsmith's poems.

19. *Circled.* Like "went round" just below.

22. *Sleights.* Dexterous feats. The word is rarely used now, except in the phrase "sleight of hand." Cf. *Macbeth*, iii. 5: "distilled by magic sleights;" Spenser, *F. Q.* i. 7, 30: "In yvory sheath, ycarv'd with curious slights;" *Id.* v. 9, 13: "slights and jugling feates," etc.

25. *Simply.* In a simple manner, artlessly.

27. *Mistrustless.* Unconscious, having no suspicion.

28. *Titter'd.* An onomatopoetic word. H. p. 218. Cf. *giggle*, which means a slightly different kind of laughter.

29. *Sidelong.* "Probably the *long* is a corruption of the adverbial termination *ling*, which yet survives in *grovelling* and *darkling*" (Hales). Shakes. (*Temp.* ii. 1) has *flatlong*, with which cf. Spenser, *F. Q.* v. 5, 18: "Tho with her sword on him she flatling strooke."

35. *Lawn.* Here used almost in the same sense as "plain," line 1.

37. *Amidst.* Some modern editions have *amid*, but Goldsmith always uses *amidst.*

40. *Stints thy smiling plain.* "Deprives thy plain of the beauty and luxuriance that once characterized it" (Hales).

42. *Works its weedy way.* A good example of "alliteration's artful aid." H. p. 298.

44. *The hollow-sounding bittern.* Cf. *An. Nat.* vol. vi.: "Those who have walked on an evening by the sedgy sides of unfrequented rivers must remember a variety of notes from different water-fowl; the loud scream of the wild goose, the croaking of the mallard, the whining of the lapwing, and the tremulous neighing of the jack-snipe. But of all these sounds there is none so dismally hollow as the booming of the bittern.... I remember in the place where I was a boy, with what terror this bird's note affected the whole village."

51. *Ill fares the land*, etc. Cf. 295. The repetition of *ill* is probably, as Hales suggests, one of the "negligences of style" that are common in Goldsmith's writings.

52. *Where wealth accumulates.* Cf. *V. of W.*: "Wealth in all commercial states is found to accumulate; the very laws may contribute to the accumulation of wealth, as when the natural ties that bind the rich and poor together are broken," etc.

54. Cf. Gower, *Conf. Am.*:

> "A kynge may make a lorde a knave;
> And of a knave a lorde also."

Also Burns, *Cotter's Sat. Night:* "Princes and lords are but the breath of kings;" and again, in the familiar song:

I

"A prince can mak a belted knight,
    A marquis, duke, and a' that;
    But an honest man's aboon his might,
    Guid faith, he mauna fa' that."

59. *Her.* "Labour" is personified as feminine.   H. p. 146.
63. See on 17.   Cf. 81 below.
65. See on 35.
67. The first ed. has "to luxury allied."
70. Cf. Carew, *Disdain Returned:* "Gentle thoughts and calm desires."
74. *Manners.*   See on *Trav.* 127.
77. For this and the three following lines the first ed. has the couplet,

" Here as with doubtful, pensive steps I range,
    Trace every scene, and wonder at the change."

83. See extract from Irving, p. 123.
86. *Lay me down.*   For the pronoun see on *Trav.* 32.
87. *Husband out.*   Economize.   Cf. the use of the noun in *Macbeth,*
ii. 1 : "There's husbandry in heaven; their candles are all out."   The
addition of "out" is peculiar.   Wordsworth in one passage has "to
husband up The respite of the season."
93. *An hare.*   See on *Trav.* 34.   *Whom* for *which* is an inaccuracy not
uncommon in British writers even in our day.   On *hounds and horns* cf.
Shakes. *T. A.* ii. 3 : "Whiles hounds and horns and sweet melodious birds.".
94. *She flew.*   Thus in the early editions; not "he flew," as in some
modern reprints.
95, 96. Forster remarks : "This thought was continually at his heart.
In his hardly less beautiful prose he has said the same thing more than
once, for, as I have elsewhere remarked, no one ever borrowed from
himself oftener or more unscrupulously than Goldsmith did.   'A city
like this,' he writes in letter ciii. of the *Citizen of the World,* 'is the soil
for great virtues and great vices. . . . There are no pleasures, sensual or
sentimental, which this city does not produce ; yet, I know not how, I
could not be content to reside here for life.   There is something so se-
ducing in that spot in which we first had existence, that nothing but it
can please.   Whatever vicissitudes we experience in life, however we
toil, or wheresoever we wander, our fatigued wishes still recur to home
for tranquillity : we long to die in that spot which gave us birth, and in
that pleasing expectation find an opiate for every calamity.'   The poet
Waller, too, wished to die 'like the stag where he was roused.' "
99. *How happy he.*   The first ed. has "How blest is he," which is re-
tained by some of the recent editors.   On *crowns* cf. 85.
102. Cf. *The Bee:* "By struggling with misfortunes we are sure to re-
ceive some wound in the conflict : the only method to come off victorious
is by running away."
104. *Tempt the deep.*   A Latinism.   Cf. Virgil, *Ecl.* iv. 32 : "temptare
Thetim ratibus."
107. *His latter end.*   A common Bible phrase.   Cf. *Num.* xxiv. 20, *Job*
viii. 7, *Prov.* xix. 20, etc.
109. *Bends to the grave.*   The reading of the 4th, 7th, and other early
editions.   Some have "Sinks to the grave."

111, 112. The rhyme is the same as in 95, 96.

116. *Mingling.* Sometimes incorrectly printed "mingled." The succeeding lines are a good example of the "correspondence of sound and sense." Campbell's *Philos. of Rhet.* pp. 340-349.

121. *Bay'd.* Cf. Shakes. *J. C.* iv. 3 : "I had rather be a dog, and bay the moon," etc.

122. *The vacant mind.* Cf. Shakes. *Hen. V.* iv. 1 :

> " Can sleep so soundly as the wretched slave,
> Who, with a body fill'd, and vacant mind,
> Gets him to rest," etc.

124. Cf. *An. Nat.* vol. i. : "The nightingale's pausing song would be the proper epithet for this bird's music."

As the nightingale is not found in Ireland, the introduction of the bird here is either a Hibernicism or a poetic license. Cf. Byron, note on *Siege of Corinth :* "I believe I have taken a poetic license to transplant the *jackal* from Asia. In Greece I never saw nor heard these animals ; but among the ruins of Ephesus I have heard them by hundreds."

129. This woman is said to have been Catherine Giraghty, or Geraghty. See p. 127, footnote.

130. *Plashy.* Puddle-like. Wordsworth has "the plashy earth." .See Wb.

135. See on 17.

137. This description of the "village preacher" was written soon after he received the tidings of his brother Henry's death, and bears traces of the recent grief. Irving says : "To the tender and melancholy recollections of his early days awakened by the death of this loved companion of his childhood we may attribute some of the most heartfelt passages in his *Deserted Village.* Much of that poem we are told was composed this summer, in the course of solitary strolls about the green lanes and beautifully rural scenes of the neighbourhood ; and thus much of the softness and sweetness of English landscape became blended with the ruder features of Lissoy. It was in these lonely and subdued moments, when tender regret was half mingled with self-upbraiding, that he poured forth that homage of the heart rendered as it were at the grave of his brother. The picture of the village pastor in this poem, which we have already hinted, was taken in part from the character of his father, embodied likewise the recollections of his brother Henry ; for the natures of the father and son seem to have been identical. In the following lines, however, Goldsmith evidently contrasted the quiet settled life of his brother, passed at home in the benevolent exercise of the Christian duties, with his own restless vagrant career :

> 'Remote from towns he ran his godly race,
> Nor e'er had changed, nor wished to change his place.'

To us the whole character seems traced as it were in an expiatory spirit ; as if, conscious of his own wandering restlessness, he sought to humble himself at the shrine of excellence which he had not been able to practise."

142. *Passing.* Surpassingly, exceedingly ; once a common word in this sense.

Cf. the Dedication to *The Traveller :* "a man who, despising fame and fortune, has retired early to happiness and obscurity, with an income of forty pounds a year."

143. Cf. *Heb.* xii. 1.

145. *Unpractis'd.* The 1st ed. has "Unskilful;" and in 148, "More bent to raise," etc. The use of the infinitive ("to fawn" for "in fawning ") is a Latinism. Cf. 161, 195, 288, etc.

149. See on 17.

152. Cf. Hall, *Satires :* "Stay till my beard shall sweep mine aged breast."

153. *Spendthrift.* One of an expressive class of words, most of which are obsolete; as *scapethrift* (Holinshed), *wastethrift* (B. and F.), *dingthrift,* that is, one who " dings " or drives away thrift, as in Herrick (quoted by Nares):

> " No, but because the dingthrift now is poore,
> And knowes not where i' th' world to borrow more."

155. *The broken soldier.* Cf. Campbell, *Soldier's Dream :* " And fain was their war-broken soldier to stay ;" also Virgil, *Æn.* ii. 13 : "fracti bello ;" and xii. 1 : "infractos adverso Marte."

171. *Parting life.* See on 4.

176. *Accents.* For words, as often in poetry. Cf. Longfellow, *Excelsior :*

> " And like a silver clarion rung
> The accents of that unknown tongue."

178. Cf. Dryden, *Good Parson :* " His eyes diffused a venerable grace."

180. Cf. Jasp. Mayne, *Mem. of Ben Jonson :*

> " For thou e'en sin didst in such words array,
> That some who came bad parts went out good play ;"

and Dryden, *Brit. Red. :*

> " Our vows are heard betimes, and Heaven takes care
> To grant before we can conclude the prayer ;
> Preventing angels met it half the way,
> And sent us back to praise who came to pray."

182. *Steady zeal.* It is "ready zeal " in the 1st and some modern editions. Goldsmith doubtless changed it on account of the "ready smile," three lines below.

189. Lord Lytton (*Miscellaneous Works*, vol. i. p. 65) has traced this simile to a poem by the Abbé de Chaulieu, who lived 1639–1720, and whose verses were popular at the time when Goldsmith was travelling on the Continent :

> " Tel qu'un rocher dont la tête
> Egalant le Mont Athos,
> Voit à ses pieds la tempête
> Troublant le calme des flots,
> La mer autour bruit et gronde ;
> Malgré ses émotions,
> Sur son front élevé règne une paix profonde."

" Every one," adds Lord Lytton, " must own that, in copying, Goldsmith wonderfully improved the original, and his application of the image to the

Christian preacher gives it a moral sublimity to which it has no pretension in Chaulieu, who applies it to his own philosophical patience under his physical maladies."

194. *Unprofitably gay.* An English friend writes : "Goldsmith was wrong when he wrote this line. The furze is not *unprofitable.* The cottager knows how to use it. The green young species give food to horse and cow, or donkey maybe, and its old branches make a first-rate fence."

196. *The village master.* Goldsmith is supposed here to have drawn the portrait of his own early teacher, of whom Irving gives the following account :

"At six years of age he passed into the hands of the village schoolmaster, one Thomas (or, as he was commonly and irreverently named, Paddy) Byrne, a capital tutor for a poet. He had been educated for a pedagogue, but had enlisted in the army, served abroad during the wars of Queen Anne's time, and risen to the rank of quartermaster of a regiment in Spain. At the return of peace, having no longer exercise for the sword, he resumed the ferule, and drilled the urchin populace of Lissoy."

After quoting lines 193–216, Irving adds :

"There are certain whimsical traits in the character of Byrne, not given in the foregoing sketch. He was fond of talking of his vagabond wanderings in foreign lands, and had brought with him from the wars a world of campaigning stories, of which he was generally the hero, and which he would deal forth to his wondering scholars when he ought to have been teaching them their lessons. These travellers' tales had a powerful effect upon the vivid imagination of Goldsmith, and awakened an unconquerable passion for wandering and seeking adventure.

"Byrne was, moreover, of a romantic vein, and exceedingly superstitious. He was deeply versed in the fairy superstitions which abound in Ireland, all which he professed implicitly to believe. Under his tuition Goldsmith soon became almost as great a proficient in fairy lore. From this branch of good-for-nothing knowledge, his studies, by an easy transition, extended to the histories of robbers, pirates, smugglers, and the whole race of Irish rogues and rapparees. Everything, in short, that savoured of romance, fable, and adventure was congenial to his poetic mind, and took instant root there; but the slow plants of useful knowledge were apt to be overrun, if not choked, by the weeds of his quick imagination.

"Another trait of his motley preceptor, Byrne, was a disposition to dabble in poetry, and this likewise was caught by his pupil. Before he was eight years old Goldsmith had contracted a habit of scribbling verses on small scraps of paper, which, in a little while, he would throw into the fire. A few of these sibylline leaves, however, were rescued from the flames and conveyed to his mother. The good woman read them with a mother's delight, and saw at once that her son was a genius and a poet. From that time she beset her husband with solicitations to give the boy an education suitable to his talents."

198. *Truant.* The original meaning of this word (see Wb.) was vagabond, but it is found in this special schoolboy sense in Shakes. *M. Wives*, v. 1 : "Since I plucked geese, played truant, and whipped top, I knew not what 'twas to be beaten till lately."

200. *Disasters.* The word originally meant the baleful aspect of a star or planet; from the Latin *dis* and *astrum.* Cf. *Hamlet,* i. 1: "Disasters in the sun." Other words of astrological origin are *mercurial, jovial, saturnine, ascendency, influence, ill-starred,* etc.

203. *Circling round.* Cf. "circled" in 19.

205, 206. *Aught* and *fault* are an imperfect rhyme, but Pope has used a similar one :

> "Before his sacred name flies every fault,
> And each exalted stanza teems with thought."

It is said that in Ireland, Scotland, and some parts of England, the sound of the *l* is often omitted in the pronunciation of *fault.*

207. *Village.* For villagers, by metonymy. H. p. 85. Cf. Ovid, *Fasti,* ii. 655: "Conveniunt celebrantque dapes vicinia supplex."

209. *Terms and tides.* The former refers to "the sessions of the universities and law courts;" and the latter to "times and seasons" (Hales). Cf. Shakes. *K. John,* iii. 1: "Among the high tides in the Calendar;" that is, solemn seasons. *Noontide, eventide, springtide,* etc., are still in use, at least in poetry.

210. *Gauge.* That is, measure the capacities of casks.

218. *Forgot.* See on *Trav.* 358.

221. *Nut-brown.* A simile compressed into one word. Cf. Milton, *L'Allegro,* 100: "Then to the spicy nut-brown ale." The word is also applied to a brunette complexion, as in the famous old ballad of "The Nut-brown Maid."

226. *Parlour.* From the French *parler,* and meaning originally the speaking-room in a monastery—that is, the room where conversation was allowed. See Wb. Cf. *boudoir* from the French *bouder,* to pout.

228. *Click'd.* Onomatopoetic. See on "titter'd," 28.

232. *The twelve good rules.* These were, "1. Urge no healths; 2. Profane no divine ordinances; 3. Touch no state matters; 4. Reveal no secrets; 5. Pick no quarrels; 6. Make no comparisons; 7. Maintain no ill opinions; 8. Keep no bad company; 9. Encourage no vice; 10. Make no long meals; 11. Repeat no grievances; 12. Lay no wagers." These rules were ascribed to Charles I. Goldsmith, in the fragment describing an author's bedchamber, speaks of them as "the twelve rules the royal martyr drew."＊ Cf. Crabbe, *Parish Register :*

> "There is King Charles and all his golden rules,
> Who proved Misfortune's was the best of schools."

＊ This fragment, which was afterwards worked over in this passage of *The Deserted Village,* first appears in a letter to his brother Henry, written in the early part of 1759, from which the following is an extract:

"*Y*our last letter, I repeat it, was too short; you should have given me your opinion of the design of the heroi-comical poem which I sent you. You remember I intended to introduce the hero of the poem as lying in a paltry ale-house. You may take the following specimen of the manner, which I flatter myself is quite original. The room in which he lies may be described somewhat in this way:

> 'The window, patch'd with paper, lent a ray
> That feebly show'd the state in which he lay;
> The sanded floor that grits beneath the tread,
> The humid wall with paltry pictures spread;

The royal game of goose. Not the ordinary game of "fox and goose," but an obsolete game played upon a board with sixty-two compartments. It is described in Strutt's *Sports and Pastimes*, bk. iv. ch. 2. "It is called the game of goose because at every fourth and fifth compartment in succession a goose was depicted ; and if the cast thrown by the player falls upon a goose, he moves forward double the number of his throw."

234. See description of Mr. Hogan's "restored" ale-house, p. 127, footnote.

235. *Chimney.* That is, the fireplace. Cf. Milton, *L'Allegro*, 111: "And stretch'd out all the chimney's length ;" and Shakes. *Cymb.* ii. 4 : "the chimney Is south the chamber." See Wb.

239. *Obscure it sinks.* Sinks into obscurity.

240. Cf. Horace's address to the wine-jar (*Od.* iii. 21) : " addis cornua pauperi ;" and Burns, *Tam O'Shanter :*

> "Kings may be blest, but Tam was glorious,
> O'er a' the ills o' life victorious."

243. *The barber's tale.* The garrulity of barbers had passed into a proverb.

244. *Woodman,* which now means a wood-chopper, used to mean a hunter. Cf. *Merry Wives*, v. 5 : "Am I a woodman, ha? speak I like Herne the hunter?"

248. *Mantling bliss.* The foaming cup, "which maketh glad the heart ;" an instance of metonymy. Cf. Pope : "And the brain dances to the mantling bowl ;" and Tennyson, *In Memoriam*, civ. : "Nor bowl of wassail mantle warm." For the different meanings of *mantle* (cf. 132) see Wb.

250. *Kiss the cup.* Just touch it with her lips. Cf. Scott, *Marmion*, v. 12 : "The bride kissed the goblet, the knight took it up."

252. See on 17. Cf. 320 and 337.

258. Cf. Milton, *P. L.* ii. 185 : "Unrespited, unpitied, unrepriev'd ;" iii. 231 : "Comes unprevented, unimplor'd, unsought ;" v. 899 : "Unshaken, unseduc'd, unterrified ;" Shakes. *M. of V.* iii. 2 : "Is an unlesson'd girl, unschool'd, unpractis'd ;" Byron, *Childe Harold :* "Without a grave, unknell'd, uncoffin'd, and unknown," etc.

259. *Pomp.* In its original sense of train or procession. See Wb.

265. *Survey.* That is, observe. The omission of the infinitive sign *to* in the next line is exceptional.

The game of goose was there expos'd to view,
And the twelve rules the royal martyr drew ;
The Seasons, fram'd with listing, found a place,
And Prussia's monarch show'd his lamp-black face.
The morn was cold : he views with keen desire
A rusty grate unconscious of a fire ;
An unpaid reckoning on the frieze was scor'd,
And five crack'd teacups dress'd the chimney board.'

* * * * *

"All this is taken, you see, from nature. It is a good remark of Montaigne's, that the wisest men often have friends with whom they do not care how much they play the fool. Take my present follies as instances of my regard. Poetry is a much easier and more agreeable species of composition than prose ; and, could a man live by it, it were not unpleasant employment to be a poet."

268. *An happy land.* See on *Trav.* 34. Cf. *Cit. of World,* i. : "there is a wide difference between a conquering and a flourishing empire."

274. *Products.* Not "product," as in some editions.

275 foll. See introductory remarks, p. 124. Cf. Horace, *Od.* ii. 15, for a similar complaint that the rich man's palaces, ponds, etc., occupy lands once productive and useful. See also *Od.* ii. 18, 19–28.

279. Note the transfer of "silken" from "robe" to "sloth." H. p. 86.

280. Cf. 40 above.

283. He seems to mean that the country exports more than its surplus productions, bartering for foreign luxuries what it really needs for home consumption.

285, 286. We follow the punctuation of the early editions. It is often printed thus :

> "While thus the land, adorn'd for pleasure all,
> In barren splendour feebly waits the fall."

287. This use of *female* for "woman" is now properly considered a vulgarism.

288. *Secure to please.* Confident of pleasing. See on **145.** Cf. Thomson, *Autumn,* 202 :

> "Veil'd in a simple robe, their best attire,
> Beyond the pomp of dress; for loveliness
> Needs not the foreign aid of ornament,
> But is when unadorn'd adorn'd the most."

293. *Solicitous to bless.* Anxious to charm, or "to find lovers on whom she may bestow her favours."

295. *Thus fares the land.* Cf. 51 above.

297. *Verging.* As it verges, or tends.

298. *Vistas.* Views, prospects. See Wb.

299. This is the punctuation of the best editions. Some point the couplet thus :

> "While, scourg'd by famine, from the smiling land
> The mournful peasant leads his humble band."

300. Cf. Roscoe's *Nurse :* "Sinks the poor babe, without a hand to save."

304. *To scape.* This word is commonly printed as a contraction of *escape,* but we find it also in prose ; as in Bacon, *Adv. of L.* ii. 14, 9 : "such as had scaped shipwreck," etc. Shakes. uses it much oftener than *escape.* See Wb. *s. v.* Cf. *estate* and *state, esquire* and *squire, espy* and *spy, establish* and *stablish* (2 *Sam.* vii. 13 ; 1 *Chron.* xvii. 12), and similar pairs of words of Norman-French origin.

305. *Stray'd.* Having strayed. Cf. *sped* in 309.

313. The 1st ed. has "To see each joy," etc.

316. *Artist.* For *artisan,* as the latter word was sometimes used for *artist.* Dr. Johnson, in his *Dictionary,* does not recognize the specialized sense of "painter" for *artist.* Cf. Waller, *To the King :*

> "How to build ships, and dreadful ordnance cast,
> Instruct the artists, and reward their haste ;"

and, on the other hand, *The Guardian* (quoted by Hales) :

> "Best and happiest artisan,
> Best of painters, if you can,
> With your many-colour'd art
> Draw the mistress of my heart."

317. *Long-drawn pomps.* Cf. Gray's *Elegy:* "the long-drawn aisle;" and see on 259 above.

318. *Glooms.* This verb occurs again in 363, where it is used tran-sitively.

319. *Dome.* See on *Trav.* 159.

322. *Torches.* Before the introduction of street-lights, people who could afford it were preceded by torch-bearers when going abroad at night.

326. See on 287. Cf. *Cit. of World*, ii. : " These poor shivering females have once seen happier days, and been flattered into beauty . . . Perhaps now lying at the doors of their betrayers, they sue to wretches whose hearts are insensible."

335. *Ambitious of the town.* Longing for or aspiring to a city life.

336. *Wheel.* That is, spinning-wheel. Of course, *country* is an adjective, and *brown* a noun.

338. *Participate* regularly takes the preposition *in*, though *of* is sometimes used. See Wb.

342. *The convex world.* Cf. Virgil, *Ecl.* iv. 50 : " Nutantem convexo pondere mundum."

344. *Altama.* The Altamaha river, in Georgia. *To* = in response to, or in consonance with.

348. *Day.* By metonymy for the heat or light of day, as in 41. Cf. Pope, *Messiah:* " And on the sightless eyeball pour the day."

352. *Gathers death.* Collects its deadly venom.

354. *The rattling terrors.* The rattle of the rattlesnake.

355. *Crouching tigers.* The jaguar and the puma are the " American tigers."

356. Cf. Sir W. Temple (quoted by some of the editors) :

> "To savage beasts who on the weaker prey,
> Or human savages more wild than they."

358. *Mingling*, etc. Cf. Virgil, *Æn.* i. 134 :

> " Iam caelum terramque meo sine numine, Venti,
> Miscere, et tantas audetis tollere moles?"

366. *Hung round the bowers.* Some of the early editions have " their bowers."

368. *Seats.* Abodes, homes; like the Latin *sedes.* Cf. 6 above.

371. Cf. Goldsmith's *Threnodia Augustalis:* " The good old sire, un-conscious of decay."

373. *Conscious virtue.* Cf. Virgil, *Æn.* xii. 668 : " et conscia virtus."

378. The 1st ed. has " for her father's arms." The meaning of course is that she left her lover in England to accompany her father to America.

384. *Silent manliness.* Manly silence.

385. *O Luxury!* For this " third degree of personification," see H. p. 153 foll.

386. *Things like these.* " Not referring to anything in the context, but to the general subject of the poem, the innocence and happiness of country life."

391–394. Cf. *Trav.* 144.

397. *Methinks.* See on *Trav.* 283.

398. For the figure ("Vision," so-called) see H. p. 165.

399. *Anchoring.* Anchored, at anchor.

402. "He seems to distinguish between *shore* and *strand*, making *strand* mean the beach, the shore in the most limited sense of the word" (Hales).

407. See on 385.

409. *Unfit.* Unsuited; not from any fault or defect in herself, but because the times are degenerate.

413. Cf. Wither's address to the Muse in *The Shepherd's Hunting:*

> "And though for her sake I'm crost,
> Though my best hopes I have lost,
> And knew she would make my trouble
> Ten times more than ten times double,
> I should love and keep her too,
> Spite of all the world could do.
>
> * * * * * * *
>
> She doth tell me where to borrow
> Comfort in the midst of sorrow,
> Makes the desolatest place
> To her presence be a grace,
> And the blackest discontents
> To be pleasing ornaments.
>
> * * * * * * *
>
> Therefore, thou best earthly bliss,
> I will cherish thee for this—
> Poesy, thou sweet'st content
> That e'er heaven to mortals lent." etc.

416. *Fare thee well.* In this expression *thee* probably = *thou.* See Abbott, *Shakes. Gr.* 212.

418. *Torno's cliffs.* There is a river Tornea (or Torneo, as it is sometimes written) flowing into the Gulf of Bothnia, and forming part of the boundary between Sweden and Russia. There is also a Lake Tornea in the extreme northern part of Sweden. Cf. Campbell: "Cold as the rocks on Torneo's hoary brow." *Pambamarca* is said to be a mountain near Quito.

419. *Equinoctial fervours.* Equatorial heat.

422. See on *Trav.* 176.

423. In some of the earlier editions, the couplet is punctuated thus:

> "Aid slighted Truth; with thy persuasive strain
> Teach erring man to spurn the rage of gain."

The "my" for "thy" in some editions is obviously a misprint.

424. *Rage of gain.* Rage for gain; Seneca's "lucri furor."

426. *Very blest.* A violation of the rule that *very* cannot be joined to participles; though *blest* here may be regarded as an adjective.

427. The last four lines, Boswell tells us, were added by Dr. Johnson.

428. *Mole.* A mound or breakwater at the mouth of a harbour. Cf. Cicero, *De Off.* ii. 4: "moles oppositae fluctibus;" Horace, *Od.* iii. 1: "Jactis in altum molibus."

430. *Rocks.* That is, natural rocks, as opposed to the artificial "mole." *The sky* = the weather, like the Latin "caelum."

RETALIATION.

THIS poem was the last work of Goldsmith, and was not printed until after his death, appearing for the first time on the 18th of April, 1774.

The following account of the origin of the poem is from the original manuscript in Garrick's handwriting, and was first printed in Cunningham's edition of Goldsmith :

" As the cause of writing the following printed poem called *Retaliation* has not yet been fully explained, a person concerned in the business begs leave to give the following just and minute account of the whole affair :

"At a meeting* of a company of gentlemen, who were well known to each other, and diverting themselves, among many other things, with the peculiar oddities of Dr. Goldsmith, who never would allow a superior in any art, from writing poetry down to dancing a hornpipe, the Doctor with great eagerness insisted upon trying his epigrammatic powers with Mr. Garrick, and each of them was to write the other's epitaph. Mr. Garrick immediately said that his epitaph was finished, and spoke the following distich extempore :

> 'Here lies Nolly Goldsmith, for shortness call'd Noll,
> Who wrote like an angel, but talk'd like poor Poll.' †

Goldsmith, upon the company's laughing very heartily, grew very thoughtful, and either would not or could not write anything at that time ; however, he went to work, and some weeks after produced the following printed poem called *Retaliation*, which has been much admired, and gone through several editions. The public in general have been mistaken in imagining that this poem was written in anger by the Doctor : it was just the contrary ; the whole on all sides was done with the greatest good humour ; and the following poems in manuscript were written by several of the gentlemen on purpose to provoke the Doctor to an answer, whicn came forth at last with great credit to him in *Retaliation.*"

As Cunningham suggests, the above was " evidently designed as a preface to a collected edition of the poems which grew out of Goldsmith's trying his epigrammatic powers with Garrick."

Irving, after giving the history of the poem, comments upon it as follows :

" The characters of his distinguished intimates are admirably hit off, with a mixture of generous praise and good-humoured raillery. In fact the poem for its graphic truth, its nice discrimination, its terse good-

---

* At the St. James Coffee-House in St. James Street.
† This couplet has been printed in a variety of forms, but this is doubtless the correct one, as we have it on Garrick's own authority.

sense, and its shrewd knowledge of the world, must have electrified the club almost as much as the first appearance of *The Traveller*, and let them still deeper into the character and talents of the man they had been accustomed to consider as their butt. *Retaliation*, in a word, closed his accounts with the club, and balanced all his previous deficiencies.

"The portrait of David Garrick is one of the most elaborate in the poem. When the poet came to touch it off, he had some lurking piques to gratify, which the recent attack had revived. He may have forgotten David's cavalier treatment of him, in the early days of his comparative obscurity; he may have forgiven his refusal of his plays; but Garrick had been capricious in his conduct in the times of their recent intercourse: sometimes treating him with gross familiarity, at other times affecting dignity and reserve, and assuming airs of superiority; frequently he had been facetious and witty in company at his expense, and lastly he had been guilty of the couplet just quoted. Goldsmith, therefore, touched off the lights and shadows of his character with a free hand, and, at the same time, gave a side hit at his old rival, Kelly, and his critical persecutor, Kenrick, in making them sycophantic satellites of the actor. Goldsmith, however, was void of gall even in his revenge, and his very satire was more humourous than caustic.

"This portion of *Retaliation* soon brought a retort from Garrick, which we insert, as giving something of a likeness of Goldsmith, though in broad caricature:

> 'Here, Hermes, says Jove, who with nectar was mellow,
> Go fetch me some clay—I will make an odd fellow:
> Right and wrong shall be jumbled, much gold and some dross,
> Without cause be he pleased, without cause be he cross;
> Be sure, as I work, to throw in contradictions,
> A great love of truth, yet a mind turn'd to fictions;
> Now mix these ingredients, which, warm'd in the baking,
> Turn'd to learning and gaming, religion and raking.
> With the love of a wench let his writings be chaste;
> Tip his tongue with strange matter, his lips with fine taste;
> That the rake and the poet o'er all may prevail,
> Set fire to the head and set fire to the tail;
> For the joy of each sex on the world I'll bestow it,
> This scholar, rake, Christian, dupe, gamester, and poet.
> Though a mixture so odd, he shall merit great fame,
> And among brother mortals be Goldsmith his name;
> When on earth this strange meteor no more shall appear,
> You, Hermes, shall fetch him, to make us sport here.'

"The charge of raking, so repeatedly advanced in the foregoing lines, must be considered a sportive one, founded, perhaps, on an incident or two within Garrick's knowledge, but not borne out by the course of Goldsmith's life. He seems to have had a tender sentiment for the sex, but perfectly free from libertinism. Neither was he an habitual gamester. The strictest scrutiny has detected no settled vice of the kind. He was fond of a game of cards, but an unskilful and careless player. Cards in those days were universally introduced into society. High play was, in fact, a fashionable amusement, as at one time was deep drinking; and a man might occasionally lose large sums, and be beguiled into deep potations, without incurring the character of a gamester or a drunkard.

Poor Goldsmith, on his advent into high society, assumed fine notions with fine clothes; he was thrown occasionally among high players, men of fortune who could sport their cool hundreds as carelessly as his early comrades at Ballymahon could their half-crowns. Being at all times magnificent in money matters, he may have played with them in their own way, without considering that what was sport to them to him was ruin. Indeed, part of his financial embarrassments may have arisen from losses of the kind, incurred inadvertently, not in the indulgence of a habit. 'I do not believe Goldsmith to have deserved the name of game-ster,' said one of his contemporaries; 'he liked cards very well, as other people do, and lost and won occasionally; but as far as I saw or heard, and I had many opportunities of hearing, never any considerable sum. If he gamed with any one, it was probably with Beauclerk, but I do not know that such was the case.'

"*Retaliation*, as we have already observed, was thrown off in parts, at intervals, and was never completed. Some characters, originally intend-ed to be introduced, remained unattempted; others were but partially sketched—such was the one of Reynolds, the friend of his heart, and which he commenced with a felicity which makes us regret that it should remain unfinished:

> ' Here Reynolds is laid, and, to tell you my mind,
> He has not left a wiser or better behind;
> His pencil was striking, resistless, and grand;
> His manners were gentle, complying, and bland;
> Still born to improve us in every part,
> His pencil our faces, his manners our heart.
> To coxcombs averse, yet most civilly steering,
> When they judg'd without skill he was still hard of hearing;
> When they talk'd of their Raphaels, Correggios, and stuff,
> He shifted his trumpet and only took snuff.
> By flattery unspoil'd'——

"The friendly portrait stood unfinished on the easel; the hand of the artist had failed."

1. *Scarron.* Paul Scarron, "the creator of French burlesque," born at Paris 1610, died in 1660.

5. *Our dean.* Dr. Thomas Barnard, a native of Ireland, made Dean of Derry in 1768; afterwards Bishop of Killaloe, and transferred from that see to Limerick. Cumberland (see line 9), in some verses published after *Retaliation* appeared, attempted to apply to wines the characters which Goldsmith had appropriated to dishes, and called Dr. Barnard "a bump-er of conventual sherry." The Dean replied to his two friends in some verses, of which the following formed the conclusion:

> "Your venison's delicious, though too sweet your sauce is—
> Sed non ego maculis offendar paucis.
> So soon as you please, you may serve me your dish up,
> But, instead of your sherry, pray make me—a bishop."

Our younger readers may miss the pun in the last line unless we inform them that "bishop" was the name of a beverage made of wine, oranges, and sugar.

6. *Our Burke.* Edmund Burke, the eminent statesman and orator (1728–1797). Dr. Johnson said of him: "The mind of that man is a perennial stream ; no one grudges Burke the first place."

7. *Will.* William Burke, a kinsman of Edmund, who said of him, "He has nothing like a fault about him that does not arise from the luxuriance of some generous quality." He was for a time in the House of Commons, and held various public offices at home and in India.

8. *Dick.* Richard Burke, a younger brother of Edmund, and a barrister.

9. *Cumberland.* Richard Cumberland (1732–1811), a man of versatile ability, but not eminent in any one department of literature. He wrote essays, pamphlets, poems, plays, novels, etc.

10. *Douglas.* Dr. John Douglas (1721–1807), a Scotchman and a celebrated controversialist of that day. He afterwards became Bishop of Carlisle, and later of Salisbury.

11. *Garrick.* David Garrick (1716–1779), the famous actor.

14. *Ridge.* John Ridge, a member of the Irish bar, whom Burke described as "one of the honestest and best-natured men living, and inferior to none of his profession in ability." His name does not occur again in the present poem.

Reynolds. Sir Joshua Reynolds (1723–1792), the great English painter. See the Dedication of *The Deserted Village,* etc.

15. *Hickey.* Thomas Hickey, an eminent Irish attorney, known in the club as "honest Tom Hickey."

16. *Gooseberry fool.* A dish made of gooseberries and cream. See Wb.

23. *The good dean.* See on 5 above.

29. *Edmund.* Burke ; see on 6.

34. *Tommy Townshend.* A well-known member of Parliament of that day, afterwards Lord Sydney. See 88.

38. *Nice.* Scrupulous.

43. *Honest William.* See on 7.

45. [Is there a confusion of metaphors in this passage ? H. p. 111.]

51. *Honest Richard.* The "Dick" of line 8. He broke a leg in 1767, to which accident the poet alludes just below.

62. *The Terence of England.* An example of the figure known as antonomasia. H. p. 84. The allusion to the Latin dramatist needs no explanation.

67. *Dizen'd.* The more common word is *bedizened.*

63. *A rout.* That is, an evening party.

86. *Our Dodds,* etc. Dr. William Dodd was a fashionable preacher of the time, and noted also as a writer. He came to a bad end, being executed for forgery in 1777.

William Kenrick was a dramatist and reviewer, and had given lectures on Shakespeare. He hated Goldsmith, and had often attacked him anonymously. Irving speaks of him as "Goldsmith's constant persecutor, the malignant Kenrick."

87. *Macpherson.* James Macpherson (1738–1796), a Scotchman, who in 1762 published poems attributed to Ossian, "founded in part on Gae-

lic traditional poetry, but so modern in form and expression of the senti-
mental gloom then fashionable, that they owed their great success to the
reproduction in new form of living tendencies of thought" (Morley).

89. *Lauders and Bowers.* William Lauders, a Scotchman and a school-
master, was the author of a famous literary forgery. He wrote a series
of papers charging Milton with plagiarism, but Dr. Douglas (see on 10)
showed that the passages quoted in proof of the charge were fictitious.
Archibald Bower was another Scotchman, who published a "History of
the Popes," full of errors and plagiarisms, which were exposed by Dr.
Douglas.

115. *Ye Kellys and Woodfalls.* Hugh Kelly was an Irishman, and a
writer of essays, poems, and plays. Johnson used to speak of him as a
man who had written more than he had read. As a dramatist he was
regarded as Goldsmith's chief rival, and when *She Stoops to Conquer* had
taken the town by storm, the following epigram appeared in the news-
papers :

> "At Dr. Goldsmith's merry play,
> All the spectators laugh, they say;
> The assertion, sir, I must deny,
> For Cumberland and Kelly cry.
> *Ride, si sapis.*"

Another, addressed to Goldsmith, alludes to Kelly's early apprentice-
ship to stay-making :

> "If Kelly finds fault with the *shape* of your muse,
> And thinks that too loosely it plays,
> He surely, dear Doctor, will never refuse
> To make it a new *Pair of Stays!*"

William Woodfall was the editor of the *Morning Chronicle*, a leading
paper of the time, and was especially famous as a theatrical critic.

116. *Commerce.* "Interchange of flattery and compliments."

117. *Grub-street.* Now Milton Street,* in London. In the 17th and
18th centuries it was a favourite haunt of literary men, but as its respecta-
bility declined it became the home of a crowd of inferior authors—poor
in a double sense—who hid from the bailiffs in its old-fashioned houses
and dingy courts. Hence the name of Grub-street came to be a synonym
for that class of writers.

118. *Be-Roscius'd.* Lauded as a second Roscius, or as the rival of the
greatest of Roman actors.

124. *Beaumonts and Bens.* Francis Beaumont (1586–1615), associated
with John Fletcher as joint author of thirty-eight plays. The *Bens* al-
ludes of course to "rare Ben Jonson" † (1573–1637).

125. *Hickey.* See on 15.

131. *Flat.* "Having no opinion of his own."

138. The reading in some eds. is "a better or wiser."

---

* When the name was changed we do not know. Milton's tomb is in the church of
St. Giles, Cripplegate, close by ; and the sites of his house in Barbican, and of his birth-
place in Bread Street, Cheapside, are both within a few minutes' walk.

† The inscription on the tablet to his memory in Westminster Abbey was "O rare
Ben Jonson," but when the stone was "restored" some years ago it was made to read
"O rare Ben Johnson," and the blunder has been allowed to stand.

145. *Raphaels, Correggios.* That is, paintings by those masters ; one of the most familiar forms of metonymy. H. p. 86.

146. *He shifted his trumpet.* Reynolds was so deaf that he had to use an ear-trumpet. Cf. *La Vie de Le Sage:* "Il faisait usage d'un cornet qu'il appeloit son bienfaiteur. Quand je trouve, disoit-il, des visages nouveaux, et que j'espère rencontrer des gens d'esprit, je tire mon cornet; quand ce sont des sots, je le resserre et je les défie de m'ennuyer."

147. *By flattery unspoil'd.* The manuscript of the poem ended with this broken line. It was probably the last that Goldsmith wrote.

POSTSCRIPT.

There seems to be no doubt that these lines are Goldsmith's, though they were not made public till some time after the rest of the poem.*

1. Caleb Whitefoord, a native of Edinburgh, came to London in early life, and was for some years a wine-merchant. A man of varied attainments and of facetious disposition, he was a favourite with authors and artists, and a frequent writer of both prose and verse under assumed names. To the *Public Advertiser* he contributed humourous letters, "mistakes of the press," and "cross-readings." He wrote some epitaphs on Goldsmith, Cumberland, and others, which were so sarcastic as to offend his friends ; whereupon he wrote an apology, of which the last stanza reads thus :

> " For those brats of my brain
> Which have caus'd so much pain,
> Henceforth I'll renounce and disown 'em ;
> And still keep in sight
> When I epitaphs write:
> *De mortuis nil nisi bonum.*"

2. *A grave man.* "Whitefoord was so notorious a punster that Dr. Goldsmith used to say it was impossible to keep him company without being infected with the itch of punning."

14. The quotation is from *Hamlet,* v. 1 : "Your flashes of merriment that were wont to set the table on a roar."

16. *Woodfall.* His friend, Mr. H. S. Woodfall, the editor of the *Public Advertiser.*

---

* In the 7th edition of *Retaliation* (London: 1774) the "Postscript" is introduced by the following note:

"After the fourth Edition of this Poem was printed, the Publisher received an Epitaph on Mr. Whitefoord, from a friend of the late Doctor Goldsmith, inclosed in a letter, of which the following is an abstract.

'I have in my possession a sheet of paper containing near forty lines in the Doctor's own hand-writing: there are many scattered, broken verses, on Sir Jos. Reynolds, Counsellor Ridge, Mr. Beauclerk, and Mr. Whitefoord. The epitaph on the last-mentioned gentleman is the only one that is finished, and therefore I have copied it, that you may add it to the next edition. It is a striking proof of Doctor Goldsmith's good-nature. I saw this sheet of paper in the Doctor's room, five or six days before he died ; and, as I had got all the other Epitaphs, I asked him if I might take it. "*In truth you may, my Boy,* (replied he) *for it will be of no use to me where I am going.*" ' "

INDEX OF WORDS EXPLAINED.

K

CPSIA information can be obtained at www.ICGtesting.com
Printed in the USA
BVOW031031080513

320219BV00001B/85/A